THE A–Z OF TRUST LEADERSHIP

NEIL BLUNDELL

SERIES EDITOR: ROY BLATCHFORD

JOHN CATT
FROM HODDER EDUCATION

To order, please visit www.johncatt.com or contact Customer Service at education@hachette.co.uk / +44 (0)1235 827827.

ISBN: 978 1 0360 0498 9

© Neil Blundell 2024

First published in 2024 by
John Catt from Hodder Education,
An Hachette UK Company
15 Riduna Park, Station Road,
Melton, Woodbridge IP12 1QT
www.johncatt.com

Typeset in the UK.

Printed in the UK.

A catalogue record for this title is available from the British Library.

This book is dedicated to my leadership team, including the core leadership group and board. Most have been with me from the beginning and it has been a privilege to co-create the organisation, learning so much along the way.

ACKNOWLEDGEMENTS

My thanks go to the wider system leadership who have been so generous in sharing their material and hard work.

Thanks to Carl for Zugzwang.

CONTENTS

Section Two

FOREWORD

The politics, pitfalls and possibilities of schools working closely together have been a feature of our national system of education for as long as it has existed. Yet the ambitions of 21st-century governments to deliver a so-called trust-led landscape are far removed from the 1944 Education Act's original vision of schooling in this country. There is nervousness in the system.

Stand back a while. Let us ponder the word 'trust'.

This five-letter word has its origins in the Old Norse word *traust*: a safe abode, confidence, security. The Vikings brought the word to England in the 800s. We have been playing with it ever since.

Interestingly, the Mercers, Haberdashers and Skinners – to name three philanthropic organisations involved in education today – were established in the 14th and 15th centuries as distinguished livery companies, a reflection of their guild and trading origins. The Charitable Uses Act of 1601 enshrined in law the idea of a list of purposes or activities that 'the State believed were of general benefit to society, and to which the State wanted to encourage private contributions'.

Charitable trusts gathered momentum in the 19th century with the advent of hundreds of cooperatives across Europe. Today, according to the organisation Pro Bono Economics, the UK charity sector contributes a mammoth £200 billion in economic value each year, many times the official estimate. It is a thriving part of the economy, and brings much to society's wellbeing.

A trust conveys something soft and not-for-profit; an entity that speaks of cooperation, collegiality and working for the greater good.

The notion of academy trusts, alongside hospital trusts, is a more recent one, launched by Tony Blair's government in the 1990s. And immediately this enduringly trusted word 'trust' somehow became an object of suspicion. Memorably, Robin Cook, one of Blair's cabinet members, lamented that the advent of competing NHS trusts meant surgeons no longer shared best medical practices.

Over the past 20 years, the abuses in governance and finance that have been a regrettable feature of the multi-academy landscape – albeit in a tiny minority of cases – have reinforced the view that trusts are in some way dodgy.

How sad this is. Every teacher knows that great teaching is rooted in trusting relationships with students. Every leader knows that great schools are founded upon trusting professional relationships.

In shaping the partnership/trust-led landscape ahead, all stakeholders must commit to transparency and work in good faith with others. The system's collective ambition must surely be to create families of schools that benefit those within and beyond their boundaries. A culture of *traust* must be the bedrock. Ego-driven competition between trusts has to be a feature of the past landscape. Rebecca Boomer-Clark of Academies Enterprise Trust speaks rightly of 'system generosity'.

Trust is, of course, a word that lies at the centre of our personal lives. A breakdown of trust in a relationship or family is a torpedo to the heart. Most of us as humans have experienced that feeling. And no organisation can escape human error. So let the coming decade in education be one in which, by 2030, we can sing the praises of a partnership/trust-led system run for the benefit of children and young people's wellbeing and academic achievements, led by professionals who are proud to serve.

In common with all titles in this series, Section One is ordered under the A–Z alphabetical headings. Section Two presents further material for professional development.

What Neil Blundell succeeds in writing – taking the reader from **Balderdash** and **Dividend**, through **Mistakes** and **Pedagogy**, to **Wonga** and **Yellow** – is an outstanding analysis of the current multi-academy landscape, and how we got here.

His advice and provocations on culture, autonomy, scale, standardisation, civic responsibility, governance, capacity and the future add up to a compelling handbook for leaders of any partnerships or groupings of schools.

Roy Blatchford, series editor

INTRODUCTION

Every day feels like the first day, and every day you think, 'They're going to fire me; I don't know what I'm doing here; I don't know how to do this; I don't know why I'm here; everybody's going to find out.'

Michelle Williams

It is not just leaders in education who are reluctant to put themselves forward, hampered by self-doubt and working on the assumption that most people know more than they do. Some time ago, I began meetings with local multi-academy trust (MAT) CEOs in an attempt to share learning and work towards a more sustained partnership. The meetings were productive and cordial but often left me feeling somewhat overwhelmed.

I found that I would return to our central team musing about the things that we had not done and perhaps should have done. The team no doubt began to dread my return from the CEO gatherings.

It took an impromptu and candid conversation in a pub sometime later for a few of us to realise that we all similarly left these meetings feeling like we had too much to do; like we had not made enough progress. The truth was that we were all doing stuff – important stuff – it just wasn't the same stuff, and we all made each other feel like it might not be the right stuff.

This book is written in the spirit of that conversation and, several years on, I am still not always sure that we are doing the right stuff. I am, however, more comfortable with that now. Looking back, I can see the progress we have made. There are many different ways to set up and run

9

a multi-academy trust; to dictate one correct way would be to ignore the diverse range of circumstances that leaders find themselves within and the differing local nuance and politics.

Nevertheless, there has been learning in this presently immature system. This is an attempt to share some of our experiences and challenges along the way. If I had read it seven years ago, it would have been a help to me as I hope it might be to others.

I draw from my own experience of setting up a multi-academy trust in the South West of England; from one school serving approximately 900 students to a growing, and significantly larger, network of children and young people. My perspectives are drawn from experiences in small- and medium-sized trusts and reflections about the role or challenges for large trusts are merely conjecture, not born out of personal involvement.

Neil Blundell

https://www.cathedralschoolstrust.org/

SECTION
ONE

SECTION
ONE

ABOUT

When we look for information about a school or multi-academy trust, our first stop is often the 'About Us' section of the website. In the early part of my education leadership career, I didn't pay too much attention to this. Preparing for school visits during school improvement or inspection work, I would often sit in the reception, looking vaguely at the values and vision emblazoned on the wall or take note of the glossy PR brochure peppered with soundbites.

'Aspire', 'Challenge', 'Ambition', 'Kindness', 'Hope', 'Courage' – it all seemed a little vacuous to me; moreover, it often didn't represent the culture that I found in the school I was visiting, reviewing or inspecting. Children and staff seemed, all too often, unaware of what these words really meant or, indeed, how the words applied to their daily lives. Sometimes the school lacked the very kindness, ambition or courage represented in the statements. Looking back, it seems odd that I was so cynical or ambivalent about cultural statements. When working in schools, I often used Haim Ginott's well-known passage:

> I have come to a frightening conclusion.
>
> I am the decisive element in the classroom.
>
> It is my personal approach that creates the climate.
>
> It is my daily mood that makes the weather.
>
> As a teacher I possess a tremendous power to make a child's life miserable or joyous.
>
> I can be a tool of torture or an instrument of inspiration.
>
> I can humiliate or humour, hurt or heal.

In all situations it is my response that decides whether a crisis will be escalated or de-escalated, and a child humanized or dehumanized.

Andy Hunter quotes this passage in *The A–Z of Secondary Leadership*, also in this series, and I make no apology for repeating the message here. Twenty-five years into educational leadership, I recognise increasingly that leaders' personal approaches do create the climate and determine the weather. It took me too long to fully understand the importance of culture. My personal paradigm of leadership has shifted; for me, culture has become the most important thing for a school or, indeed, a multi-academy trust. When we get it right, culture describes who we want to be at our best; how we hope to behave. Where it works well, people in all parts of the organisation buy into it, understand it deeply and work collegiately in support.

To cite Dan Nicholls, Director of Education at the Cabot Learning Foundation:

> Strong trusts know and understand why they exist. They have a set of compelling values and clarity of purpose that galvanises colleagues into shared endeavour and collective responsibility. This clarity aligns colleagues, informs the strategic investments and paints a compelling future that guides the big and small decisions made across the trust by all colleagues every day. It is in these actions, over time, and not in the written words, that culture emerges.[1]

Multi-academy trusts have been part of the English system for more than a decade now. The MAT movement evolved from the academies' movement in the early 2000s and was accelerated after the appointment of regional school commissioners in 2014. With greater adoption of academies as a tried-and-tested educational model, and with all new schools becoming free schools, MATs have quickly become the predominant model of school governance in England. They are, however, still relatively new organisations. Although nearly half of English schools have joined or

---

1   Nicholls, D. (2023) 'Five functions of a strong trust, strong trust, great schools'. Available at: https://dannicholls1.com/2023/02/26/five-functions-of-a-strong-trust-strong-trust-great-schools/

formed one, it is still early days, and there is likely to be an ongoing debate for some time about which model best supports school improvement.

The most academised region is the South West and, despite some political 'rowing back' following the publishing of the white paper ('Opportunity for all: strong schools with great teachers for your child') in March 2022, there has been a gradual increase in academisation. Over the next decade, it seems likely that most schools within England will become part of a wider, non-local-authority-related family, and the Department for Education (DfE) has persisted with the phrase 'all schools to be in or joining a strong trust by 2030'.

In his book *The Advantage: Why Organizational Health Trumps Everything Else in Business*, Patrick Lencioni[2] states that there are six critical questions which every leader must be able to answer:

1. Why do we exist?
2. How do we behave?
3. What do we do?
4. How will we succeed?
5. What is most important right now?
6. Who must do what?

The first two questions are fundamental for all trusts, so when we look to consider 'About Us' within the MAT system, there are perhaps two things worth referencing:

Macro

1. What is the purpose of a trust? How does being part of a family of schools improve the lives of children, and how does working collaboratively improve teaching and leadership?

Micro

2. How does a trust define its vision and values? How do CEOs, trustees and leaders define their reason for being and how does this differ from a single-school context?

---

2   Lencioni P. M. (2012) *The Advantage: Why Organizational Health Trumps Everything Else in Business*. New Jersey: Jossey Bass.

My own experience of setting up a trust came about as part of the free school movement. As an existing headteacher of an academy in Bristol in 2011/12, I suggested to the governing body via the chair that we might consider setting up a primary feeder school in the second wave of the free school movement. The secondary school was a music specialist school, and we were dismayed at the lack of musical experiences children had been exposed to before starting KS3. Developing earlier musical opportunities for children, nurturing talent and providing musical experiences, particularly for the most disadvantaged children, was something that governors could see might benefit the wider community.

As a result, in 2013, our first primary school free school opened its doors to its first cohort of children. The new school temporarily borrowed some space from its secondary sister school. It had only three teachers at the outset, and we had no idea whether it was sustainable. In those days, the DfE was prepared to open schools without permanent accommodation – the race was on to find the school a home before it grew too big.

It was a stressful time. Parents had bought into the vision of the new school – they knew the risks – but it would have been heartbreaking to have had to close the school if accommodation could not be found. Ten years on and the school is thriving, with buildings next door to the secondary school and with the students from the first cohort (now in Year 10) continuing to perform, play and sing just as we imagined they would.

From 2013, we recognised the challenges of governance for two schools. We had opened another school without thinking about what might be the best structure for the future. The governors of both schools began to think about it, and three choices became apparent:

- Form an all-through school and lose precious funding.
- Form a trust and invite other schools to join us.
- Join another, more-mature trust.

A sub-group was formed and we began speaking to other trusts, considering how we might align our vision and values. It was much more complicated than anticipated; for a start, the original secondary school was a Church of England academy. Even more complicated than that, it was a 'Cathedral school'; one of the rare independent schools that had made the transition to the state sector in 2008. The diocese clearly needed to be consulted; a consultation that would result in nearly five years of debate about the right set of articles.

What became apparent was that our curriculum values were not shared across other trusts. As a pair of music specialist schools, we were anxious to ensure that music and the performing arts would continue to be promoted and encouraged. It was difficult to find reassurance that this would be protected. Things were beginning to feel complicated! Other questions began to be considered:

- Where did we see autonomy standardisation and how much choice would our school leaders have in deciding the curriculum, budget etc.?
- What about geography? What were the benefits of continuing to serve local communities?
- Size: did we want to become part of a large organisation? What scale of trust brought the most benefits for our schools?

These were all big questions, and we didn't have the answers. In short, we didn't know who we were or who we wanted to be. We didn't have confident answers to either the macro or the micro questions.

However, our thinking was developing and we were beginning to understand what was important to us. In developing the beginnings of a vision which set out some broad parameters, including size, geography and constitution, we were clear that we wanted to be part of a local trust that was not too big, that valued the performing arts and creativity, that was welcoming to different types of school (faith and non-faith) and that had high levels of autonomy. It was a start, and enough to make the decision to form our own trust.

Looking back, it is interesting to reflect on how little thought we as leaders gave to the deeper 'About Us' question. Perhaps it was not surprising. It was a busy time: encouraging other schools to join, submitting an additional secondary free school bid, trying to look after our existing schools, engaging with the diocese. It all took time and energy. In truth, the deeper 'About Us' thinking evolved over time. Our views have changed and continue to evolve. I was clearly naive in the early days, not recognising enough how the competing influences of ego, control, politics, history and, of course, existing culture all combined to form a complicated landscape which wasn't just about children and families, teaching or leadership.

So when we look at trusts, at different cultures, it is important to reflect on the 'About Us'. How does it inform us about the way the organisation leads and behaves? What about the way it treats staff and children? What is its moral purpose?

The landscape is complex and ever changing; trusts are forming and reforming, merging and closing. Not all the decisions made in the last decade were sensible. In many cases, growth was prioritised at the expense of intelligent design. There are more checks and balances in place now. However, the degree to which trusts vary is enormous, and a method for best practice across the system has not yet been widely disseminated. While we get on with that maturation project, we must recognise that there is still much to do to ensure that trusts reflect and are held to account.

The system is shifting and at different rates. In regions with fewer academies, new trusts are forming all the time and in the more mature areas, we are beginning to see mergers and acquisitions. As we do, we must ensure that the rationale for change includes a compelling vision; a vision which clearly articulates why and how the new organisation will work to benefit children and further contribute to the wider system.

ASIDE

Question

• How do trust leaders ensure that the values of the organisation are well defined, shared and evolved?

A good way of really understanding the culture of an organisation is to ask staff what they value most and what they would least like to lose. Ultimately, culture drives behaviours, decisions and processes. You can also ask colleagues what behaviours they would like to lose. When we are considering how to form or join a trust, it is the most important thing.

BALDERDASH

Many leaders now fully immersed in senior leadership within the multi-academy system have become relatively blind to the opposing position. Only half of the schools within England operate within these structures, and there are thousands of leaders who have not yet begun to explore the advantages and disadvantages of the system. Many regard the trust system as an inappropriate response to the demise of the LA (local authority) and lament the loss of school autonomy. In short, there are many who think it is *balderdash*.

Behind the cynicism, there are no doubt factors that are worth exploring in detail.

COLLABORATION

Hardwired into the system for multi-school improvement is the need to collaborate so that best practice can be disseminated and so that all schools within a family can improve together. Collaboration is hard, and not always initially popular; it requires compromise, and that is perhaps why it is so difficult. Egos often get in the way.

Subject leaders think long and hard about what works best and often want to teach materials that they are personally invested in. English teachers may want to teach a text at KS3 that they have enjoyed and that they feel they know intimately. Music teachers might choose familiar and well-liked musical stimuli that represent a particular compositional device or skill. It is difficult to compromise around the curriculum but curriculum alignment or standardisation is necessary for school improvement to work at scale. Critically, collaboration requires leaders to grasp a bigger vision. Not everyone is prepared to do that. Strong leadership is required for successful collaboration with thoughtful structures and processes. When done well, collaboration should decrease workload though staff may fear the opposite. The perception of a loss to school autonomy and power balance between schools is common and a barrier to effective collaboration.

COMMUNITIES

How do we ensure that we retain some sense of community? Is it possible that the organisation will just get too big; so big that we lose our sense of belonging and identity? Some research points to the ideal size of human communities where society functions at its best. Very large secondary schools often have more than 150 staff, and some of the largest trusts can have up to 100 schools. The largest MATs educate in excess of 30,000 children requiring over 3500 staff. As we adapt, we need to consider how we make sense of our communities; many cannot yet perceive the benefit of working at any scale – let alone 100+ schools – and remain fearful about transitioning to the multi-school system.

LEADERS AND EGOS

This scale brings elements of the corporate world: sophisticated back-office systems and highly paid executive leaders. Not all believe that this is in the best interests of children and families. We see similar criticisms within the NHS: 'too many leaders and not enough doers, teachers, doctors or nurses'. If trusts are going to continue to be the dominant system, they must be seen to improve teaching and leadership directly.

Some headteachers may have moved into the multi-academy system to forward their careers while others may fear that moving into a trust means that they will lose autonomy, power or influence. We tend not to talk about it but we should! The early part of the system saw something of a 'land grab' with trusts growing quickly and without much intelligent design. It didn't help the reputation of the system and there were those critics who understandably called it 'empire-building'. It is important not to stifle ambition, either for individuals or organisations, but when combined with ego there is a danger that the opportunities offered within the multi-school system may become corrupted in favour of individuals rather than the good of the wider community.

TIME

'I am a good teacher and I just need the time to be with my students, my school team.' 'I have been doing this for 20+ years; these things will come and go and I cannot possibly see what part I have to play.' 'My pupils need me to teach them and don't need me disappearing every week to collaborate.' These are all genuine concerns from real and committed educationalists and we have to be able to prove that collaboration saves time and makes pedagogy richer.

Recently, a head of department stopped me in a corridor to tell me how pleased they were that the collaboration work had reduced their workload: 'I used to have nine assessments to set and moderate, now I have three!' Leaders spend so much time preparing materials and curriculum content. When they leave the school or, worse still, education, staff often take that knowledge and those materials with them. The curriculum collapses, exposing the fragility inherent within a system without scale.

INCENTIVE

'We are fine as we are!' The schools within the education community that are doing well, have been served well by effective local authorities, have good 'soft' local networks and, perhaps, are better funded than others may not see the need to make any significant adjustments – and perhaps they are right. We all know that it is easier for some; the lack of equity across the system is clear. All schools have pressures but for many, they are more acute: those serving significantly disadvantaged communities, perhaps surrounded by grammar schools, underfunded, under planned admission number (PAN), in buildings in a poor state of repair, perhaps in and out of Ofsted categories. For those schools, joining a trust may be much more attractive. If you are fine as you are, there is little short-term incentive.

Of course, to a point, it is difficult to convince colleagues that trusts work when some of them don't … yet. Colleagues cannot be easily convinced if they are only looking in from afar. Six years into our work, my thinking has changed dramatically – but only because I have been so deeply involved.

SCEPTICISM AND FALSE DATA

It is interesting to note some of the resistance from unions to academisation and multi-academy trusts. In a headline, the National Education Union (NEU) quotes three 'myths about academisation':

1. Joining a MAT improves academic attainment.
2. Academisation boosts Ofsted grades.
3. Academy trusts offer more financial support and security.[3]

I am a critical fan of academies, believing that there are more issues created by slowing the academisation process than there would be in accelerating it. Yet, the three challenges are fair and we should consider them in detail. To do so, we do need to look at the assertions in a balanced way.

Point one, relating to improving attainment, cites evidence from a UCL report from 2018 that notably focuses on academic attainment rather than progress. It draws our attention to an Education Policy Institute report, published in 2018, comparing school performance and pupil improvement at every trust and local authority in England at both key stages 2 and 4. It revealed that academy chains are 'disproportionately represented' among the worst performing groups of primary schools, with 12 making it into the bottom 20.

It is hardly surprising that the primary schools represented in 2018 were under-performing, given that trusts were key drivers for school improvement. Many schools were brokered into trusts to support them in making rapid improvement. Similarly, it is likely that many schools joining trusts over time have done so because they are concerned about their capacity for school improvement – and we all know that school improvement takes time. As a result, Ofsted grades will be equally subject to variation while school improvement initiatives take time to embed.

The Local Government Association cites new analysis that purports to prove that LA-maintained schools are performing better. The NEU has commented that the report 'demonstrates the value of a democratically organised and supported school system'. It is a debate that is likely to continue; however the issue is not whether trusts are better than

---

3   National Education Union. Available at: https://neu.org.uk/advice/your-rights-work/
     academisation/neu-case-against-academisation

LA systems. The critical question is rather: what are the best structures – governance, leadership etc. – in support of school improvement?

In relation to financial security, the NEU cites a study which found that, compared with local-authority-maintained schools, academies spent proportionately less on teacher salaries (1.5%) and educational support (1%), and more on back-office costs (1%). The study was completed in 2015–16. It will be good to look at this again in 2025–26 to see what has happened to the back-office costs and to consider whether that offers better value for money within trusts.

Although some trusts have clearly made a difference and have improved outcomes and standards at scale, others have failed to do so. The system is immature, and we are now realising that to make a difference there are several contributing factors to successful trusts. Ultimately, the difference between trusts and local authorities will be tested over time. We all know that LAs gave rise to considerable variation in standards, but had decades to prove they were the best vehicle for school improvement. The trust system needs to be given time before we say 'balderdash'.

There are various other facts cited as anti-MAT propaganda:

- Joining is irreversible. (*Mostly true, but some movement is now happening between trusts; 176 academies moved trusts in 2021–22. In my view we should have more movement between trusts. If schools do not feel they are being supported well then there should be a mechanism for carefully considered re-brokering.*)
- MATs are less accountable to parents etc. (*Not sure why this would be true, except perhaps where local governance arrangements have been significantly changed.*)
- Students are more likely to be taught by an unqualified teacher. (*Highly unlikely and I'm not sure whether there is much of an evidence base for this. Just because trusts have the freedom to appoint unqualified teachers doesn't mean they would want to.*)
- By becoming an academy, a school risks losing vital LA support. (*Not sure there is much support in some regions, though mostly LAs now work thoughtfully in true partnership with MATs.*)
- Teacher pay is worse in academies but CEO pay is soaring. (*Not convincing; all schools need to be competitive. CEO pay is clearly*

an issue. However, if a trust has 1000 employees and a turnover of £70+ million, then we should consider the appropriate remuneration the office deserves given the levels of responsibility.)

- Academies undermine staff pay and conditions. (*Really? All schools need to recruit and retain successfully. Why would we undermine pay and conditions? It would make us less competitive and that wouldn't make sense. Recruitment and retention has never been more important. To be competitive, trusts need to attract and recruit the best staff.*)

Leading within the system that is evolving requires us to be patient and to know what the critics believe. Trust leaders need to be aware of the criticisms and the shortfalls, recognising the constant need to make the case. It seems unlikely to me that well-run trusts cannot do a better job than LAs who had conflicting priorities and often a distinct lack of meaningful intervention. Some schools might argue that they go faster alone, but they might be better going further together!

ASIDE

Question

- How does the LA system better support collaboration or dissemination?

It is interesting that some of the opposition seems to follow political lines and there is an assumption that the system is a Conservative policy. In fact, the academy movement was originally a Labour policy and, as yet, there seem to be no plans for radical change by governments of any political colour. Perhaps the debate should focus on the best system to support schools irrespective of party politics and the overarching question we are seeking to answer:

What are the best structures, governance, leadership etc. in support of school improvement?

CHURCH

THE HISTORY OF CHURCH SCHOOLS

Most church schools came about through the drive for mass provision of Christian education for the poor in the early and middle years of the 19th century. The National Society for Promoting the Education of the Poor in the Principles of the Established Church, now known as The National Society (Church of England) for Promoting Religious Education (or more often simply the National Society), was created in 1811, with the mission of founding a church school in every parish in England and Wales.

By the time of the UK Census of 1851, the church had established 17,000 schools. State provision for public education came with the 1870 Education Act by supplementing the provision of the church. This Act demonstrated the partnership between the state and the church in education, and this has continued to the present day. At the beginning of the 20th century, there were over 14,000 voluntary schools, of which rather more than 1000 were Roman Catholic, with a similar number provided by the Wesleyans and other denominations. The majority of the rest were Church of England schools.

The Education Act of 1944 gave church schools the option of increased state funding and control as 'voluntary controlled schools' or lesser state support and greater independence as 'voluntary aided schools'. This Act also required that all schools have a daily act of collective worship and religious instruction. By the 1950s and 1960s, the Roman Catholic Church had expanded its school provision vigorously, especially at the secondary level. By comparison, the expansion in Anglican secondary schools was modest, and the number of its primary schools declined.

FAITH SCHOOLS IN THE MODERN SCHOOL SYSTEM

Now, a third of schools in the UK are faith schools. In 2019, faith schools made up around 34% of all state-funded mainstream schools, but the majority (6179) are primary schools, compared with only 623 secondary schools. To further complicate the picture, these numbers are made up of both voluntary aided (VA) and voluntary controlled (VC) schools. Most VC schools have 25% diocesan representation on the governing body, and VA schools have a governing body made up of a majority of diocesan representation. Admissions further complicate the picture with some VA schools having faith as part of the admissions criteria.

Adding further complexity, the Catholic schools (always a majority model) have their own politics! It is a lot to understand but if trust leaders are going to make sensible decisions, then they need to appreciate these significant nuances. In 2016, the National Society (NS) attempted to do so with a memorandum of understanding written in collaboration with the DfE that set out to establish the principles which faith schools should consider when looking at academisation, joining or forming a trust. The NS and DfE published another memorandum of understanding in September 2023.

The church has been wrestling with interpretation for centuries, and this subject guidance proved to be no exception, with different dioceses interpreting and responding to the guidance differently.

MIXED TRUSTS

Some dioceses were anxious to encourage academisation, recognising that many smaller (and sometimes isolated) church schools required the support of a local trust. Where this was the case, many set up liberal memoranda of understanding and their establishing principles allowed and often encouraged VC, and occasionally VA, church schools to join mixed MATs, asking only that they have minority articles (25% of the board represented from the diocese either selected or ratified). Some dioceses allowed VA schools to join trusts with minority articles but the position on this varies throughout the country.

Our experience was not so easy, and the process took a very long time to agree. A number of emerging trusts found similar difficulties, with dioceses asking mixed MATs (those with both church and non-church schools within them) to adopt majority articles. The question, as ever, is why? I remember vividly being told in a meeting that it was expected that our trust should become a 'church-led MAT'. I didn't really know what it meant – none of us did!

Being a mixed trust was important to us, in part because we could see positives in allowing schools and MATs to represent the complexities of society. If our school communities represent the wider society we live in, will it not be easier to encourage mutual respect and understanding? If we have schools within the family that are made up from different communities, will we not be able to share more widely our vision of what inclusive education should be?

We still operate within a system where geography defines inclusion and we know that the fractures in society in part exist because people tend to coalesce around familiarity, choosing areas to live where they feel a sense of belonging and surrounding themselves with other people like them. Where we have admissions policies which focus on the local geography, it supports the green agenda but it is at odds with inclusion and equity.

Thus, over time schools and school systems have evolved to represent the communities that they serve. In some regions, schools are often separated on religious grounds in a community which is already segregated, such as Northern Ireland. The system can be further divided over ability (the grammar school system) which some might argue adds further division. In a country where society is divided, one might question whether it is healthy to separate children further, deepening those divisions so inherent in the community.

Faith schools have universal values that we can all subscribe to, and faith schools within a trust have the potential to influence the values of the whole organisation in a positive way.

Importantly, the trust must protect the individual ethos of each school as well as ensuring that standards are maintained and improved. If the system didn't have significant variation of performance or quality, then there would be little for the church to be concerned about. In practice, that is not the case – and there are trusts that have not performed particularly well in relation to 'distinctiveness'. Standards may have declined, and values may not have been 'lived'. Where this is the case, the diocese has limited powers of intervention, having only 25% representation on the board where mixed-trust articles have been agreed.

The Statutory Inspection of Anglican and Methodist Schools (SIAMS) system is designed to alert the diocese to schools where Christian distinctiveness is not being promoted or progressed. The framework is a thoughtful one and most schools find it supportive and useful. However, there are limited and rarely used consequences for schools or trusts who are not upholding the values or standards expected within the framework; this gives little reassurance that there is a follow-on mandate for improvement. SIAMS is the Church of England and Methodist Church's outworking of the requirements of section 48 of the Education Act 2005.

ACCOUNTABILITY AND THE FUTURE OF THE OFSTED INSPECTION MODEL

How, then, should we move forward? Ultimately, the challenge for MAT and church leaders seems to centre around accountability. The current Ofsted framework is under considerable scrutiny, with many calling for the removal of the grading system. Amanda Spielman, the former Chief Inspector, has suggested that this would be a 'natural evolution' and the current Labour Party politicians and school leaders are calling for significant reform, including removing judgements. In part, this is due to the pressure within the system; there are real challenges over recruitment and retention of the workforce, and the pressures are considerable.

In January 2023, the death of Ruth Perry (a primary school headteacher who took her own life after Ofsted downgraded her school from outstanding to inadequate) made national headlines and resulted in increased calls for the system to be overhauled. For the first time in my career, I find myself in agreement. The system has not kept pace with the multi-school system and is adding considerable pressure to schools who are facing increased challenges post pandemic. Judgements about school performance should take into account multiple factors including data, the wider context and, most importantly, culture.

There is a clear need to ensure that all parties have confidence that distinctive values will be supported, developed and upheld both within individual schools and across the MAT. It is rare that a single person in any school holds the brief to uphold/support the faith distinctiveness. It is also rare that this brief is held across a trust.

It seems obvious that the quality assurance should now begin to focus on trusts, and it is clear that the pilot trust inspections have started too slowly. It is not too difficult to envisage how a new accountability framework might better serve the system and reassure stakeholders that external quality assurance is taking place, safeguarding values and improving outcomes. It is also clear that the current framework will not fit within the multi-school system.

For too long, Ofsted reports have been beige documents written to ensure that complaints cannot be made, written for the audience of parents; they are, often, unhelpful documents for schools. If single-word judgements were removed, then reports could once again nuance what schools and trusts need to do to improve. Clearly, we need to know whether safeguarding and leadership are effective or not. If not, intervention must take place, and that should provide reassurance to all that the trust or school will be required to improve and will be monitored regularly and effectively. In short, the 'special measures' judgement must surely remain. Ultimately there is a difference between punitive and supportive accountability.

Schools and trusts have to be accountable, and we know that there will continue to be a good deal of variation. If grading became binary (effective or ineffective), then schools and trusts judged as effective might be given rich developmental advice from an experienced and supportive HMI team. Furthermore, if SIAMS protocols were woven into any new accountability framework or could trigger a full inspection, this might give reassurance to all stakeholders – including the church – that there is a clear mechanism for intervention. As a result, we would not be so anxious about articles of association. Mixed MATs could be credited with effective governance without the need to be, necessarily, church-led or controlled.

Recently, the National Society released a document entitled *Our hope for a flourishing schools system: Deeply Christian, serving the common good.* In it, the society lays out its vision for all church schools. In September

2020, the National Secular Society published a paper entitled *Power grab: Academisation and the threat to secular education.*

Pluralism is integral to our modern society and our school system. If school systems do not reflect the society in which we exist, then how can we teach our children about our fundamental values? As MAT leaders, we should be aware of the diverse nature of the system – a system that has evolved over centuries. How we interpret that and work with a diverse group of MATs and other agencies will define our leadership. Meanwhile, English schools remain divided and representative of the society that has evolved.

ASIDE

The way in which we interpret both mixed and equality articles, and most importantly develop trusting relationships, is one of the most important elements of the changing system. While leaders consider next steps, they would do well to think carefully about what is in the best interests of children who have only one chance of an education. Decisions about governance and representation need to be made quickly and, if possible, consistently. In reaching some intelligent solutions, there are some key questions that we need to ask ourselves:

Questions for trust leaders

- How will the system ensure that the vision and values of all schools can be well protected within the multi-school system?
- How would the system be different if the church had lost all influence within the sector?
- Why do most diocesan bodies insist on minority, majority or equity representation?
- Is governance in the trust made stronger by the adoption of equity or majority articles?

Questions church authorities might ask of trusts and themselves

- How does the vision of the trust resonate with the school's theologically rooted Christian vision in a way that enhances the work of the school and its Christian foundation?
- How does being part of the trust enhance the school's curriculum?
- How does the trust contribute to and enhance the school's worship and spiritual life?
- How does the trust contribute to and enhance the inclusion and wellbeing of pupils and adults, ensuring that all are treated well?
- How does the trust make a positive impact on the culture of the school?
- How do school and trust leaders ensure that the provision, profile and priority of religious education in all key stages reflect its place on the curriculum of a church school?
- How do school and trust leaders ensure that the religious education curriculum is challenging, accurate, well-sequenced, well-balanced, relevant and diverse?
- How do school and trust leaders ensure that religious education is well-resourced, and that continuing professional development for staff has an impact on the effectiveness of the curriculum?
- What decision is in the best interests of our children and families?
- What is more important: stronger articles or school improvement?

DIVIDEND

What is the trust dividend? In other words, what difference does it make when we work in collaboration? As trusts develop over time, it is more and more important to ensure that they make a difference.

Trust dividend = A significant and persistent level of performance that is contingent on the existence of the trust and enables schools to work in a higher-performance space over time. There are several things one might expect to see in effective organisations that would demonstrate that we have made a difference. How might we then define the 'trust dividend'?

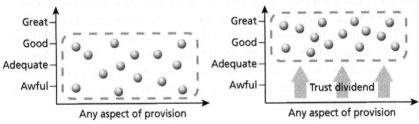

The difference made by the trust dividend (reproduced with permission, source: Dan Nicholls, 'Seeking a trust dividend: Exploiting the power of collaboration').

The trust dividend, then, can only be considered by activities that single schools cannot do.

The dividends within this system come from:

1. collaboration leading to the dissemination of best practice
2. standardisation resulting from this dissemination

3. prioritisation facilitated by back-office functions being taken away from school leaders

4. talent management; the ability at scale to draw on the wider talent pool.

It has always struck me as rather odd that we seem to measure ourselves against international comparisons where the conditions, societal norms and culture are widely different. Politicians talk about Pisa comparisons and occasionally lament our poor international standing when compared with, for example, Norway or Singapore. That is not to say that we should not attempt to compare ourselves with the highest-performing systems across the globe but it seems akin to measuring inner city deprived schools against leafy grammar or independent schools. It is apples versus pears.

The most important thing to agree on is what we value most so that we can develop success criteria in relation to that.

The same is true for the measure of national success which is so often determined by economic growth. It seems that as a species, we have not yet managed to consider how continued economic growth and development sit alongside the needs of the global ecosystem; we have not yet considered how we might live well and look after the planet at the same time. There is a parallel here for the school system: how can we move forward, improving together and demonstrating dividend, without damaging the existing system? If trusts are to prove themselves, they must demonstrate their achievements against a clear set of carefully thought-through criteria. Otherwise, we are comparing fruit again, and that is no help to anyone.

EDUCATIONAL OUTCOMES

If trusts are to prove successful, then we should see outcomes for children improve. However, the measurement of improvement is likely to be proportionate to the quality of trust and sector leadership. There are plenty of trusts that have formed without really centralising systems or disseminating best practice. In short, they have formed as relatively loose federations. Over time, they may find it difficult to prove their effectiveness in terms of sustained school improvement.

The concern for many of us is that in disseminating and collaborating, we might restrict creativity. If greater alignment is the secret to ensuring all schools reach a benchmark threshold (perhaps a good or better Ofsted rating), then how do we ensure that there is enough ingenuity to move towards truly outstanding practice? There is a danger that through alignment we might stifle creative pedagogues and talented leaders. Setting the conditions for these sorts of behaviours to flourish is therefore critical.

We should assume that well-led trusts will evoke positive progress in relation to the most commonly used measures. At secondary level, Progress 8 is an attempt to define a standard measure of achievement against national benchmarks. However, it is a relatively blunt measure, and we recognise the issues. Despite the lack of contextualised information, we should expect to see well-run trusts performing well against KS2, 4 and 5 measures and, over time, avoiding the significant in-school and in-trust variations in outcomes. Post pandemic has become more difficult to compare value added, with significant gaps in data and teacher-led assessments getting in the way. The recent widening of the disadvantage gap has made it even more difficult for those trusts made up, predominantly, of schools with high levels of disadvantage to demonstrate dividend.

If the MAT system is to demonstrate value added then schools should become less fragile over time in relation to educational performance and with less variability. There are those who continue to compare academies with LA-led schools and, while this is an important thing to do, we should avoid hyperbole, bias and clumsy misuse of data.

EDUCATIONAL OPPORTUNITIES

Any attempt to quantify the input and output of schools has its flaws. We know that the quality of a child's education is often measured too simply and in terms of academic outcome only.

Increasingly, there is an attempt to measure other benefits/dividends which contribute to wider student development including cultural capital. Michael Young's description of 'powerful knowledge' has generated much attention over recent years and we all recognise that the most disadvantaged students need to be supported so that they are better able to explain and understand the natural and social worlds, they can engage in current debates of significance and, importantly, they can go beyond the limits of their personal experience. Developing the co-curricular entitlement for children is, therefore, an important part of ensuring some sort of individual educational dividend for every child.

So often, the disadvantage gap can be measured in relation to a lack of opportunity. How, then, can we ensure that collaboration can provide enhanced opportunities for children? Many trusts consider the provision of co-curricular opportunities alongside the curriculum, in some instances tracking a series of entitlements that all children within the family of schools will receive over time. So where trusts have some form of all-through provision, staff have constructed a series of opportunities that all will access: going to the theatre, playing in an ensemble, singing in a choir, cooking a meal for friends, climbing a mountain. These opportunities are designed to be age appropriate and woven around the core curricula. How the trust work supports those wider developmental opportunities is therefore also important to quantify.

FINANCIAL SECURITY

Within highly centralised systems, we should assume that part of the dividend will be related to value for money. Achieving scale should improve our buying power, and resilience. Having a larger budget with larger reserves gives greater flexibility and enables trusts to think a little more creatively about projects and over time. Whether the trust reserves are 'pooled' or not, there is an inherent safety net in the system. When schools go into deficit, the general reserves of the trust support them and this in-built sense of collegiality can give reassurance to headteachers and governing bodies that they have time to sort the budget. It also acts as an incentive when schools realise that they cannot and should not be using the reserves from other schools in this way. In effect, the financial dividend should be noticed in terms of resourcing, be it via capital or student-focused resources.

TALENT MANAGEMENT

Scale should give rise to opportunities to promote, retain and redeploy good people around the system. As a result, we should be stronger and the people element to 'dividend' should be felt by schools. Ultimately, schools have different performance metrics when compared with other institutions, and these metrics are sometimes more difficult to quantify. Schools do well when they have good teachers and good leadership; it is a simple and complementary formula. If the dividend is apparent, then strong trust staff should feel that there are opportunities for them within their trust.

How then do trust leaders ensure that teaching and leadership improve with scale, maximising the talent? Trusts that grow and, through that growth, invest in leadership development, pedagogical coaching, collaboration and dissemination activities should reap the dividend by improving teaching and leadership and developing talent, thus fulfilling potential.

How we measure the leadership and teaching dividend is worth considering. One of the questions to ask leaders at the beginning of the academic year is relevant here. Is the quality of teaching and leadership capacity stronger this September than last? It is an obvious question but rarely considered by governing bodies or trust boards. If the answer is yes and that is replicated over a number of years, then the school is likely to be moving forwards rather than backwards; there is no such thing as a school in stasis. If the capacity for teaching and leadership is weaker, then the trust must intervene as there will likely be little dividend. Measuring the quality of leadership over time is much more difficult to do, but we should make the attempt.

CIVIC RESPONSIBILITY

We can all think of examples of schools that are totally dependent on external support and cannot thrive on their own. We also know that all too often strong, wholly-inward-looking schools, that were often geographically close by, contributed little or nothing to their struggling neighbours.

In a competitive system, this is understandable; being oversubscribed at the expense of the school down the road that may have diminishing numbers on roll is a moral dilemma. Having better outcomes, be they value added or otherwise, can lead, via admissions in a competitive market, to improved and better budgets and facilities. Schools with better budgets and facilities may find recruitment and retention easier. It is a destructive cycle in a competitive system and all headteachers are aware of that tension. Established trusts should be aware that they have an increasingly moral obligation to 'do no harm', to take their fair share of challenging schools and play their part.

Trusts have an in-built consideration for other members of their family and this helps to support the system as a whole. They are beginning to work more widely across areas. However, they can and should play a wider role in society.

The opportunity for trusts to work with other civic partners adding a wider dividend is something that is beginning to emerge. For example, trusts are working actively with local authorities on place planning and SEND (special educational needs and disabilities) strategies, complementing the statutory duties of local authorities. Working collaboratively with NHS services and charities, using schools as community hubs and resource centres, providing holiday and weekend care in partnership – all of this is emerging across the system and trust leaders, particularly in the larger organisations, should and are thinking altruistically, seeing the dividend as wider than their own schools and wider than the school system.

Civic work has the most impact when it is done in partnership with other civic actors. There will be some areas where it makes sense for trusts to take the lead while in others, specialists may be better placed to make connections and develop partnerships. The evolution of trusts is not yet widely understood in other sectors and there is a danger that other 'actors' do not consider trusts when thinking about civic work. The challenge for trust leadership is to make connections and tell the story of how the system is evolving and what that means. All too often I speak to people from other walks of life who have not kept up with the changes to the school system and simply do not understand the changes that have taken place and how it all works.

How, then, do we make sure that we partner effectively with our own schools, other trusts and wider community groups to ensure that we generate lasting and secure dividend? The metrics of dividend are as yet unclear and there is limited accountability except where things go very wrong. Too often intervention occurs when it is too late and radical, expensive action is required. The point about ensuring that there are consistent quality assurance processes and measures for trusts will be made throughout and seems like an obvious next step for the system. There are some recent attempts to codify effectiveness that we will cover in later chapters.

The trust movement is still in its infancy and trying to make the case for the existence of trusts wholly via performance data is misguided. There will always be a degree of variability and, in part, that comes from the fact that many small and immature trusts have not yet realised their potential. Ultimately, it seems to come down to a single question: are schools within trusts better able to focus on school improvement when compared with schools in LA systems or stand-alone academies?

ASIDE

Questions

- How might we encourage educational leaders to take wider ownership of the system, supporting others in an era of competition?

- How should leaders collaborate across trusts and what conditions need to be in place in order for them to be fruitful?

Local authorities still have responsibility for place planning but trusts have a part to play. It may be that reducing the published admission number (PAN) of a large, four-form-entry primary school temporarily in one trust might help ensure that an under-subscribed, single-form-entry school from a competitor MAT continues to exist. Traditionally, LAs also support the finding of alternative places for students at significant risk of exclusion. Relevant alternative provision and local sharing of resources might now be better supported by trusts who may choose to collaborate to achieve scale.

While local authorities continue to have responsibility for place planning, what role should they play in the planning, opening and running of new schools? In order to ensure that MAT-system leadership develops an increasing level of civic responsibility, what incentives or direction might the DfE consider?

ENTREPRENEURS

Those who choose to work in education are rarely seen as entrepreneurs, that is, those who lead an organisation with considerable risk and initiative. Teaching and educational leadership are perhaps perceived as rather safe professions, where pensions and holidays are seen as something of an incentive. Financially, there are guarantees in the state system: places are paid for per pupil, communities need schools, and the DfE cannot afford for schools to fail. The risks are there but the opportunities for educationalists to take advantage of them are fewer than in the corporate world. There is, however, a real need for initiative, risk taking and doing things differently.

Politicians have promoted competition in schools for quite some time and with some success. Before the evolution of the trust system this had the side effect of limited collaboration. The challenge is to encourage both.

There are several factors that have led to school leaders seizing the multi-school initiative:

1. The drive from central government for decentralisation and diversification, including the free school movement.

2. A greater degree of parental choice and parental dissatisfaction with the school system.

3. Increased societal polarisation and increased post-pandemic change.

4. Developments in technology.

One might argue that the risks are, if not smaller, then certainly different in education. However, the stakes for school leaders are high, and are arguably becoming higher. We all recognise that there are large numbers of good people whose careers have stalled or worse because they have taken on risky projects, further contributing to the national debate about the pressures on school leaders exacerbated by the inspection system. School improvement and systemic change take time, and the inspection system is predicated on a fixed time and place; the here and now. There is little 'give' in the framework for conjecture and in support of school improvement over time.

There is no doubt that the conditions within education have encouraged leaders to take the initiative in pursuit of a 'self-improving school system'. Historically, educational innovation has been glacial; arguably, the practices and systems within our schools have changed little over time. The world of education continues to be rooted in the 19th century, delineated by both geography and time. We all continue to clock in and clock out in the same place within pre-set time frames established during the industrial revolution.

The relatively new understanding about how the brain works is changing our perceptions of pedagogy. During the pandemic, we were forced to work differently – utilising technology effectively for professional development, communication and teaching. We recognised the immediate benefits but, as time passed, we also came to acknowledge the downsides.

Post-pandemic, lessons continue to be learned, and fundamental to them is the understanding that children and teachers need the social element of school life. Learning is a social activity, and schools are more than merely spaces in which we deliver a curriculum. The point, therefore, is that schools are different, and the pandemic taught us that these existing structures are supportive of social learning. While we innovate, it is important to recognise that education is perhaps a little less of a blank canvas than some might have previously thought.

One of the suggested attributes of an entrepreneur is that they are able to see, perceive and act on the surrounding environment and exploit the opportunities out there. The changing education policy gives opportunities for those who are skilled at predicting, or at least quickly following, the political tides and direction. The entrepreneurial leader is someone who has the ability to see opportunities before they are visible to others and, based on her/his perception of this opportunity, to act on it in innovative and creative ways. The entrepreneurial CEO also requires the support of a visionary chair of board. Without this, little can be achieved.

In the McKinsey report of 2010 (Mona Mourshed, Chinezi Chijioke and Michael Barber) entitled 'How the world's most improved school systems keep getting better', it is interesting to note that many of the system leaders interviewed for the report were unaware of why the innovations they had made had been successful or fitted together:

> During our interviews, the leaders of improving school systems all agreed that creating improvement required discipline and constant forward momentum. However, even amongst this august group, few were certain about why they had been successful: they often did not have a 'theory of the case' about why what they did worked. Even fewer had a mental map of how all the changes they made fit together as a coherent whole. Some even thought they had just been lucky.
>
> Mourshed, Chijioke and Barber (2010)[4]

It seems that there is a new perspective which gives rise to further tension. Traditionally, the distinction between the economic and the pedagogical entrepreneur has not been clear. This tension between education efficiency and economic efficiency, between pedagogical- and business-oriented mind-sets, differs across the globe. While the American system describes the role of the high school principal as an educational administrator, the British system still references this role as education leadership.

The title of 'headteacher' is still common across England. In part, no doubt, this comes from the desire of heads to associate with where they have come from. It is still rare for headteachers to come with a business background; the vast majority have been teachers and their practice continues to be influenced by their experiences in school, in pedagogy,

---

4   Barber M., Chijioke C., Mourshed, M. (2010) *How the World's Most Improved School Systems Keep Getting Better*. Available at: https://www.mckinsey.com/industries/education/our-insights/how-the-worlds-most-improved-school-systems-keep-getting-better

with a moral purpose stemming from supporting children and families and from the desire to improve classroom practice.

Because the current trust system is predicated on partnership, on building hard-wired opportunities for collaboration, and because that is dependent on scale, there might be a perception that those who innovate within the system – the entrepreneurial pathfinders – are 'empire-building'. This term first came into being in the latter part of the last century and has come to refer to the seeking of extra power or influence for its own sake. There is, without a doubt, some truth in the perception. Not all those who have set up trusts have done so purely in the best interests of children and families. Where trusts have been formed in pursuit of ego, we might see some aspects of the following:

- Poorly-thought-through geographical structures (growth for the sake of it); often these partnerships contain high-risk schools that might be under-subscribed, too small or in a poor state of repair.

- A culture that is not underpinned by clear vision and values and a deep understanding of why we exist.

- Structures constructed on economic efficiency rather than for the benefit of teaching and leadership.

I suspect that many founding CEOs of trusts will not see themselves as entrepreneurs. Most have been successful headteachers; as such, they have had to become good at seeing, perceiving and acting on the surrounding environment, exploiting the opportunities therein. There are so many examples of where political interference and policy have incentivised education leaders to respond: local management of schools, the specialist school movement, the trust-led system, teaching schools initiatives, subject hubs. We are all conditioned to work within a highly politicised system, and this gives rise to necessary creativity and innovation, spotting opportunities and driving change where we are encouraged to do so.

As trusts grow, the entrepreneurial aspects of leadership often become distributed between the director of education or the chief operating officer (COO) and the CEO.

A large number of trusts have devised a structure in which the 'number two' in the organisation is a director of education as opposed to a COO. Increasingly, the executive roles within the structures, those that seek to instil collaboration and dissemination, are those that drive improvements in pedagogy – particularly when augmented by phase leaders in secondary and primary. The CEO is then free to seek opportunities for growth in different directions: forming wider partnerships, generating value for money, growing and telling the story of the organisation. Entrepreneurship is useful in all leadership manifestations but it is in the role of the CEO where this is most important for the organisation.

During the early phase of development in trusts, it is difficult for a single person to hold multiple portfolios – but this is often required. The resulting tension between pedagogical and economic entrepreneurship demonstrates the challenge felt before achieving scale. It is not yet clear whether trust leadership benefits most by entrepreneurial behaviours at the start-up phase, or whether this dimension is required consistently throughout. Certainly, it is something that might be considered by boards and governing bodies who are looking to recruit at any phase of the trust journey.

What leadership qualities are required for any CEO or executive leader, and at which point those qualities are required in the development of the organisation, are vital considerations.

ASIDE

Questions for governance

- What leadership qualities does the organisation need more of or less of now?
- How are we making sure that the leadership style balance is right and specific for the context of the MAT?

As the system develops and trusts ultimately get bigger, it may be that educational leadership experience becomes less important and we will see more entrepreneurial leaders emerge from outside the system. In my view the understanding of headship, the associated anxieties and challenges therein, is a benefit rather than an essential to any trust CEO.

Ensuring that education leaders have experience of the commercial world is something that we should also aspire to provide. Who would suggest that experience outside of education would not be helpful to any emerging senior trust leader? The imperative for boards to contain this type of skill set, and the relationship between board and CEO, are critical.

FREE

Free schools were first introduced in 2010 by the Conservative–Liberal Democrat coalition as part of the 'Big Society' initiative. After this time, all new schools opening had to be free schools. There is a good deal of confusion about the difference between free schools and academies; the truth is that there is very little difference. Still, they are included here because they have played a part in the evolution of some trusts, often being seen as a way to grow and innovate.

There will be different experiences across the sector. The following case studies reflect my experience and my, arguably one-sided, interpretation.

CASE STUDY ONE

I was originally attracted to the concept through the subject-specialism debate. As a headteacher of a music specialist secondary school, I had long been frustrated by the inconsistent approach to music education in primary settings, an issue that continues to this day.

The specialism movement encouraged secondary schools to self-identify as specialising in one discipline in order to increase parental choice and stimulate excellence. If children arrive in secondary school with little or no experience of music, it is much harder to become fluent. The idea that we could develop the music curriculum from early years to post-16 in an all-through setting was appealing. Specifically, we were anxious to ensure that children from disadvantaged backgrounds might access music early with enhanced opportunities to learn instruments and participate in re-creative and creative music making.

Visioning a new school – working with colleagues to construct a compelling vision and curriculum narrative – is an exciting time.

I remember an early meeting with potentially interested parents. We had little to offer other than vision, and there were so many questions that we didn't yet have answers to, not least the question of where the school would be located. In the early free school rounds, the DfE gave permission for schools to open in temporary accommodation without securing a permanent site. So with no staff, no site identified, and no experience of setting up new schools, we set off for an interview at Sanctuary Buildings in London. Critically, we had assembled a group of governors with considerable business and educational expertise, including finance and construction. This group was central to our credibility and, eventually, our success. Once through the interview stage, we began to recruit for our headteacher designate and test the admissions market.

The real pioneers in the first waves of the free school movement were the parents. So many of those parents who expressed an interest in the original vision made applications for their children. It was such a risk: a brand-new school, with no track record of success, and with no guarantee that without a permanent home the project would be viable. These parents gambled with the things most precious to them. They truly cared about education, and they really wanted something unique for their children. It felt like a huge responsibility. I vividly remember seeing them arrive on their first day, kitted out in their new uniforms, some having only just turned four. The pressure to find a permanent home was on.

The solution came out of the blue from a conversation at a civic function with the chair of the board. The secondary school was located in the city centre, next door to the Grade I listed public library, the bottom two storeys of which were being used for storage. It was a vast, cavernous area, filled with 750,000 books and a century's worth of clutter. We recognised the potential of the space and the synergy of libraries and education felt right. Ideally, the building was located right in the middle of the secondary school campus and could share some of the facilities, including play space and dining areas.

There were big issues to overcome, however, not least the lack of natural daylight. The books being stored were archived collections and not often used; on average, between six and twelve books per week were borrowed from this section! The opportunity to relocate and digitise the collection was received positively by the library leadership team. However, the idea was not well-received by some members of the public and certain politicians, and this resulted in considerable protests.

I was surprised by the reaction which seemed to be partly related to the protection of public libraries, to which I was sympathetic, but also seemed to be politically motivated by anti-academisation, anti-free school sentiment. I struggled to see the issue; we were proposing to spend a sizeable amount of capital funding to solve the perturbing problem of primary school places and, in doing so, we were going to invest in a historically significant building, improving library services in the process.

The debate seemed to be a rallying call for all those who objected to the politics; in part, this was an objection to the academies and free school movement, but it also galvanised those who felt that local services were being eroded by a Conservative government who didn't care and who were determined to undermine the role of the local authority. We were on the receiving end. I remember one public consultation event where a protester became physically aggressive; there were tears and tantrums and attempts to vilify those involved. It highlighted the many misconceptions about education exacerbated by the misinformation that found its way into the press.

It all seems rather silly now, ten years down the line. That first cohort are now in Year 11, embarking on their GCSEs, and we have had three successful Ofsted inspections. At the end of Year 6, the year group put on a production of The Lion King. The singing and all-round performance were exceptional by any standards.

The students have continued to sing and play instruments, and it still brings tears to my eyes when I see and hear them in performances. I hope that those pioneering parents are pleased with their choice and know that these projects are dependent on them.

CASE STUDY TWO

Our second free school project exemplified the challenges around partnership, and was doomed to fail from the outset. The local post-16 landscape had always suffered from considerable urban variation. As ever, the larger providers offered much more effective provision, mirroring the national picture. As in many areas, the LAs had failed to rationalise the provision and, as a result, the landscape was peppered with a number of small post-16 providers that struggled to offer the breadth of curriculum and often performed poorly.

The idea seemed like a good one: two small trusts, both with little post-16 provision, would combine to create a larger, more successful post-16 offering. The words within the bid should have been easy to write; there was a clear need for places within the city and the rationale was obvious. However, the relationships proved problematic. The two trusts and executive leads just didn't see things in the same way, and this led to conflict in almost every area: curriculum, admissions, leadership, governance structure, site, and so on. The biggest problem, however, came down to who was in charge, both in terms of the executive team and within the governance structure. It proved impossible to resolve; the two organisations were in direct competition and were not philosophically aligned.

The bid was successful and the divisions and internal politics were hidden. A site was located next door to one of the schools, and that, ultimately, put an end to the partnership. It was an amazing opportunity, but proved to be far too much of a bridge for the other trust, who insisted that the location be near to one of its schools. This understandably parochial position highlighted the challenges of partnership work in a competitive environment and it flushed out the existing divisions, giving an excuse to part ways.

In the end, the split was for the best; the two trusts would never have been able to work together productively. The leaders just didn't see things the same way, and the thinking was always partisan. Too much compromise watered down what could have been an exciting opportunity for the children and families of the city.

CASE STUDY THREE

The third project was a secondary free school that opened in 2019. It was slightly less controversial, but no less hard work. Bristol needed secondary schools, and there was a considerable place crisis and a hurry to establish more than one new secondary school.

As a result, the LA opened a tender process, inviting trusts to bid for the opportunity to work with them to open a free school. We applied but were initially unsuccessful, losing out to a bigger, more-established national trust. Our response was to submit an application anyway, highlighting the disconnect between the old and the new way of doing things. Previously, new schools were always controlled by the LA, and the presumption route they had established would have been the only option. The free school and multi-school system changed this, but not all were aware of the changes that had occurred.

I remember well announcing to the local headteacher group that we had submitted an application. There was stunned silence. Interestingly, the bidder that had applied via the LA presumption route did not manage to get their full DfE free school application in on time so in the end, we were the only local applicant. We were successful in our interview process, and eventually found a site. The school opened in 2019 in temporary accommodation, and the building was completed in July 2021, with students moving in the following September. When the children entered their building for the first time one was heard to exclaim, 'Is this all for us?'

The LA bid was re-submitted in the next round and it succeeded. However, site-finding issues led to significant delays.

Setting up free schools is hard. Freedom is a double-edged sword. It is easy to convince yourself that by taking on the challenge you would be adding capacity to the growth of your trust. In my view, it does the opposite. Setting up a free school, while a highly rewarding and exciting endeavour with rich learning for those who are involved, is not an easy short cut to growth. It is much more straightforward to work with established schools through the normal due diligence and onboarding process than it is to set up a free school from scratch. This may be an issue of scale, with larger organisations having more capacity to deliver projects, but for a smaller start-up trust, the projects have sucked capacity out of the central team and slowed down the process of growth and maturation.

I wouldn't go back and change anything that we did. We all learned a good deal, and the transition points – children arriving for their first school day, the foundations being laid, the look on the children's faces when they entered their building on day one, the first and very successful inspections – will live long in the memory.

ASIDE

New schools are a wonderful opportunity to do something positive for local communities. It is rather depressing that the amount of capital investment has diminished and become so poor. Too often, schools have life spans of 65 years and have relatively low BREEAM (Building Research Establishment (BRE) Environmental Assessment Method) status. Contractors inevitably need to make a profit and cheaper materials, systems and products are used.

Over time, saving money at the start will end up costing the system more and seems to be another example of how our short-term political system driven by changing political direction poorly serves children and society. The foundations for the school where I was first headteacher were laid in the year 1140 and it is still being used for the same purpose. The free school we set up in 2022 has a predicted lifespan of 65 years. How is this good value for money?

GROWTH

Growth and maturation is a complicated area, and there are clearly differences of opinion across the sector. There are so many nuanced questions for trust leaders to grapple with and they must consider each carefully when considering growth.

WHAT IS THE IDEAL SIZE OF A MULTI-ACADEMY TRUST?

Clearly a number of people have an opinion, and many simply don't feel that the system is mature enough to have worked that out yet. What we do know is that trusts have developed at different rates and to differing scales. Probably, it is most helpful to consider again why we are doing what we are doing and to explore some of the frustrations that led to the political change of direction.

The 1988 Education Act is perhaps the precursor to all that we see today. This was a momentous change in political direction; for the first time, schools were given autonomy over curriculum and budgets. The changes were slow at first, but this early movement away from LA control changed everything. From this point, schools experimented with new-found curriculum leadership and budgetary freedoms – but always at single-school level, never really benefiting from economies of scale or deep collaboration.

THE PAST AND THE OPPORTUNITY TO CHANGE

We all recognised that the quality of local authorities in relation to education was variable. Many garnered the respect of educationalists and other stakeholders and provided good-quality, efficient services to schools. Some did not. At large scale, it is challenging to coordinate partnership work and those authorities with hundreds of schools found it difficult to broker these partnerships and, consequently, work on school improvement often lacked coordination. LAs had competing pressures, and education was one of many challenges they had responsibility for. No matter how good the education leads were, they were always having to pay attention to local politics championing schools and education.

The problem, then, was not just one of competing priorities, but also one of scale. How do you effectively coordinate school improvement work, transition, SEND, attendance and place planning across so many schools? As trusts have grown, the same problems have become apparent: there is a lot to do within organisations and it is not always easy to ensure that improving teaching and leadership continues to be the main priority. Trust leaders would argue that education is always at the heart of the agenda existing to better serve teaching and leadership, and as a prioritisation they argue that children and teachers are better served than they might be in local authorities. Of course, the trust system suffers from the same variability that affected LAs; some are more effective than others. Additionally, as some of them grow towards a size similar to that of a small LA, the challenges of scale and coordination are replicated.

There is no doubt that size makes a difference. Some time ago, it was suggested that to become a sustainable sponsor, trusts needed to be made up of more than ten schools – something the white paper (2022) also alludes to. Also suggested at this point – and for the first time – was the total number of students (7500). This was the first time anyone had considered sustainability and scale. It was not clear how this figure was derived, but those of us who have worked to establish and grow an organisation recognise its validity.

The diagram opposite shows the current average size of academy trusts. Note that this graph shows the average size of MAT within the data set of Kreston Academies; this is higher than for the sector as a whole.

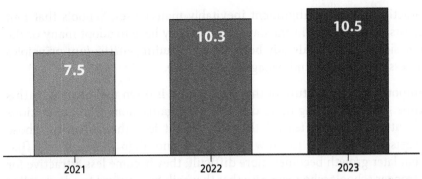

Average number of schools per MAT (reproduced from the Kreston Academies Benchmark Report, 2024).

As trusts grow, they reach points where life becomes either more or less comfortable. Inevitably, colleagues in small and growing trusts have to do more than one job. Founding leaders have to become CEOs and executive principals simultaneously. HR and finance directors have to check the minutiae. People are given lead roles on a part-time and fixed-term basis: a capable designated safeguarding lead takes on the responsibility for safeguarding across the trust or a senior leader takes responsibility for assessment and data. As the organisation grows, everybody recognises the need to focus on one job, avoiding both distractions and competing priorities. Once capable people begin to do good work, the need to support them – giving them the appropriate time and resources – becomes vitally important for the organisation. At least LAs had scale from the outset; trusts that are growing must keep evolving structures and responsibilities to keep pace with the changing needs of the organisation.

HOW SHOULD TRUSTS GROW?

Some trusts have grown very rapidly, achieving scale before maturity; others have evolved, slowly maturing as they go. There appear to be advantages and disadvantages to both. Rapid expansion gives lots of choice to new joiners in the early phase of transition; early joiners are given the opportunity to co-found: 'Come and form the organisation with us.' So many decisions have not yet been made, but the more collaboration that takes place, the more schools disseminate best practice, the more alignment inevitably materialises. Schools that join trusts relatively late in the day find that they have to adopt many of the decisions that have already been made, including curriculum principles assessment models and pedagogical practice.

Importantly, the culture of the organisation is often well formed by this time, making joining more difficult for organisations who are anxious about assimilation, fearful that they might lose their identity. Those trusts that are slow to grow but mature and align more quickly find that later growth becomes more difficult; they become less attractive for stronger schools who recognise that they will be required to adopt policy and practice.

It is certainly true that some trusts have evolved from personal relationships, formed on the basis of trust and cooperation. The rationale for partnership is, understandably, often derived from existing and personal relationships, and as a result the system is not always intelligently designed. People are much more transient than the structures they leave behind.

ARE TRUSTS BETTER AS CROSS-PHASE – PRIMARY AND SECONDARY?

Perhaps this is the issue which best highlights the differences between phases. We all recognise the divisions and lack of understanding inherent across the system and this is not just a national anomaly. Some KS3 practitioners have never set foot in a KS2 classroom, other than perhaps during their training year. Similarly, primary practitioners rarely observe at first hand what the KS3 curriculum sets out to achieve. The result is often frustration on both sides, with primary teachers lamenting the lack of focus on handwriting, for example. If/when they visit children in Years 7 and 8, I have often heard the phrase 'he/she could do better than this in Year 4'. They are right; secondary practitioners may underestimate what children know and can do when they arrive at secondary school.

This lack of understanding between primary and secondary schools persistently pervades, except in the case of a few areas with effective all-through provision and where transition comes from small numbers of local schools where good relationships have been fostered.

In reality, secondary schools often welcome children from large numbers of primary schools (up to 60 in some areas). The gaps in knowledge and understanding from KS2 are therefore different, and even harder to fill! It seems obvious that the multi-school system and cross-phase trusts might be helpful in attempting to close this gap between phases. If done well, cross-phase trusts will ensure that primary and secondary practitioners learn from each other, developing curricula that build on prior learning, intelligently sequencing to make the transition to secondary education more effective, if not quite seamless.

There is little doubt that some primary-only trusts exist in part from a concern that the larger secondaries might dominate the arena and that, as a result, the needs of primaries might not take priority. The pay gap between primary and secondary phases and the scale inherent within secondary schools may mean that there is a tendency for them to dominate the executive roles. It seems a shame that the opportunity to work more collaboratively might be lost as a result of these tensions. This is something to keep an eye on as trusts grow and merge. The cottage industry lessons continue to be learned.

The pay gap between primary and secondary means that primary-only trusts tend to have much less executive pay strain. However, getting to scale is harder and rapid growth is, therefore, more important for primary-only trusts.

As we head towards 50% of schools being in a multi-academy trust, then, it is interesting to see how this is divided up. Currently most single-phase trusts are primary, making up 33% of the system. At only 5%, it is surprising that such a small percentage of trusts are secondary only. The scales involved with secondary trusts ensure that efficiencies are easier to make. However, mixed-phase and primary-only trusts continue to dominate. Most schools are grappling with the challenge of SEND and it is understandable, therefore, that they are considering alternative and specialist provision. This is an area in which we are likely to see growth emerge within trusts.

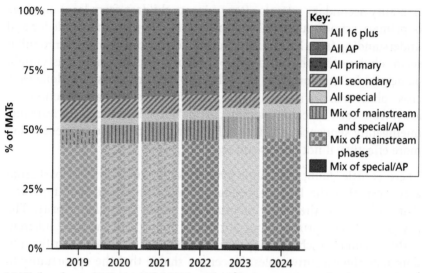

MATs by phase, 2019–24: All MATs with at least two open schools (reproduced with permission, source: FFT Education Datalab).

SHOULD TRUSTS ATTEMPT TO HAVE A CULTURALLY/SOCIO-ECONOMICALLY DIVERSE STUDENT POPULATION?

The country's school system has evolved slowly, subjected to the forces of national and local politics. We still have a system including grammar schools (163 in all); some fully selective, others partially so. The current hybrid system has proved over decades to be politically charged, with no politician prepared to face the parental voters' backlash if things were to change. Of course, we also have a strong independent school provision, with approximately 7% of the population being educated therein. So, given that the system is already partially selective and stacked in favour of the affluent and the vocal middle classes, the changes that trust leaders make in redesigning the system perhaps need to seek a better balance.

Most schools – but particularly primary schools – tend to serve local communities and, as a result, the school population is often not culturally or socio-economically diverse. The same thing has happened with trusts; those that have grown via sponsorship, effectively becoming specialists in rapid school improvement (often resulting in low levels of autonomy), have tended to become trusts which typically serve areas of high disadvantage. The truth is that not all trusts were clear about their growth parameters from the outset, and some have evolved in a rather eclectic, erratic manner. In the earlier years of the trust movement, there was something of a land grab, with the DfE clearly needing to encourage growth. Some decisions were made which, with the privilege of hindsight, we have come to regret.

In a system where the policy is to encourage rather than insist, it is not surprising that intelligent design was not the most pressing priority on the inception of the movement.

The regional directors still rely on headteacher boards which are populated from within and do not have the authority to intervene to make sense of the future or to insist on revising past mistakes. This issue is exacerbated because there is, as of yet, no formal quality assurance mechanism for trusts. The school inspectorate is piloting inspection, but it has not kept pace with the changes to the system. Where intelligent brokerage is needed, there is too little in terms of external, independent and verifiable evidence to support decisions about growth.

SHOULD TRUSTS GROW WITH A CLEAR GEOGRAPHY IN MIND?

To some extent this is a question that has already been answered – look around the landscape, locally, regionally and nationally. They didn't and that was ill thought through. We are now having to pick up the pieces.

If one of the advantages of moving away from local authority control is scale, then geography should also be important. A number of local trusts are evolving to set up satellites. Some are considering setting up groups of schools around commuting areas and motorway corridors. A portion of early adopters and large trusts have already established a national chain. Local-based trusts might extol the benefits of geographical responsiveness, acting quickly in response to the needs of headteachers and school leaders, moving staff around easily depending on where the need is.

However, larger organisations benefit from other advantages, and have proved that they can replicate success over different areas of the country. Occasionally, the lack of intelligent design or brokerage has led to some isolation, where schools have been left geographically exposed without the local support of other schools within the trust and lacking a hub or central team nearby to support them.

We now have areas where a number of local schools are supported by entirely different trusts; communities of schools that could (and perhaps should) be supporting each other, but are not. The system has led to a series of anomalies, some examples of which are listed here:

- Some primary feeder schools are in different trusts from the most local secondary school.
- There are some isolated schools whose family of other schools is not close by.
- Some schools needing support are geographically close to effective trusts but are not allowed to join them.
- There are Catholic schools that can, at present, only join Catholic trusts while VA schools can only join trusts with majority or equity articles.
- There are even instances where all-through free schools are being built with primary and secondary schools that belong to different trusts.

There is a lot to do to make sense of the last ten years of messy growth.

With all this in mind, the brokerage focus might better consider the ability of the organisation to support school improvement. When growing, trusts might give careful consideration to the following questions:

1. Is growth true to the vision and values of the organisation?
2. How will growth further our ability to support school improvement?
3. How does growth support the educational vision?
4. What will the impact of growth be on the system's local geography?
5. Do our schools recognise that during a period of growth, our capacity to support them may temporarily diminish?
6. Have we thought through the longer-term implications that growth may bring?

7. Will there be an end to growth? Have we thought about what it will look like when we get there?

There is no doubt that growth has become a metric which some use to determine the success of the organisation. This shouldn't be the case. There are plenty of trusts that have grown too quickly and then find that they do not have the mechanisms, systems or expertise to support their schools. Others have moved too slowly, exhausting leaders, missing out on opportunities and maturing systems before scale is achieved. Instead, we should think of asking a different question: what is the trust trying to achieve? In answering that question, we might then look at the scale required to achieve that aim.

I have heard a number of trust leaders say that 'big is not necessarily beautiful', although, ironically, those who say it are often in a large MAT or one entering a growth phase. Our experience is that the more collaboration and dissemination we put in place, the more trust-wide leadership roles there need to be. Doing more requires more resources, and more resources requires scale. Scale and size are different concepts, explored in a little more detail in later chapters.

Trusts often face a number of growth challenges:

- Unclear priorities about direction.
- Unclear accountability or a lack of accountability.
- Stagnant mindsets, still within the psyche of the previous organisation.
- The CEO has too many line-management reports.
- Differences of opinion between established leaders and the new strategic direction.
- The top team in critical roles are not the right talent for the new organisation.

To some extent we can always find an excuse not to grow, feeling that consolidation is more important. It is also possible that trusts can become obsessed by growth, seeing it as a sign of success. The following diagram demonstrates the recent considerable growth ambition across the sector.

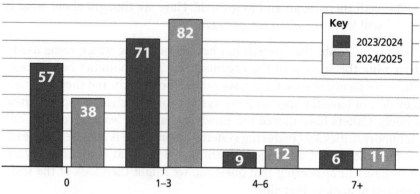

How many schools trusts are looking to grow? (reproduced from the Kreston Academies Benchmarking Report, 2024).

ASIDE

Questions for leaders

- How should leaders now make sense of the mistakes made over the last decade?
- How do we learn the lessons and share that learning across the regions as they develop?

There are some things that we know now that we didn't know ten years ago; in addition, the economic climate has changed. What constituted a resilient trust then is no longer relevant. Collections of small primary schools that are undersubscribed lack resilience; collections of schools that have little central control and too high levels of autonomy take huge risks. The only way that we can really hold trust leaders to account is to make it clear, in law, what MATs are supposed to do and to inspect to ensure quality.

HORIZONS

One of the key aspects of being a CEO that I have learned over recent years is how important it is to keep horizon-scanning and thinking about the long term. Further, we should keep challenging our own orthodoxies, considering why we are structured as we are. If some of our leadership objectives lie in sorting out some of the problems and conditions that we have created, then we should consider carefully what we want the future to look like. In doing so, we will need to consider the politics, how the system works and how we are interconnected.

It might also be helpful to look at the past, at how we got here.

In addition to church involvement in education, covered in an earlier chapter, schools have been under the control of local authorities for some time. The term was introduced by the 1902 Education Act, which designated each county council to set up a committee known as a local education authority (LEA). The councils took over the powers and responsibilities of the school boards in their area. The role of the LEA was further expanded with the introduction of school meals in 1906 and medical inspection in 1907.

The system continued largely unchanged until 1988, when one of the biggest changes since 1944 came in under the Education Reform Act: the LEAs lost responsibility for higher education, with all polytechnics and post-18 colleges becoming independent corporations. This began the break away from direct local authority control and started with the 'city technology colleges' and the 'grant-maintained schools'.

The academy movement began in the early 2000s, building on the city technology colleges of the late 1980s, ultimately evolving into the academy trust movement we see today. As we all come to terms with the changes to relationships, power dynamics, influence and politics, we are all having to adapt our thinking. There appears to be something of a slow paradigm shift occurring in education, and it is taking some time for leaders to re-conceive the way in which we respond and communicate between the DfE, LA trusts, dioceses and other partners. Similarly, and understandably, other stakeholders are unsure, lacking an understanding of the new system and how it impacts on children.

CHANGING RELATIONSHIPS

To some extent, the changing nature of relationships and changes in the way in which we work together seem inevitable, particularly while the system continues to be in flux, with some schools still overseen by LAs while others are single academies or part of a family of schools. While retaining some statutory responsibilities, LAs have had to alter their relationships with trusts and academies. Some have severed their direct links with schools and school improvement, taking the bold move to ask all schools to find a home within a given time-line. Others have retained the majority of services traditionally held by local authorities and, as a result, the local dynamics are much more competitive. Essentially, there seem to be three different types of LA:

- those where the system is fully academised
- those where the system is only partially academised and the LA is still mostly in control
- those where the system is in flux and the dynamics between LA and trusts are developing in both partnership and competition.

The uneven growth of trusts has led to a mixed provision. Some have grown quickly with less maturation, while others have matured, developing a clear sense of 'who we are' and have begun to align and develop school improvement systems at scale. Not all have found life easy, finding both growth and school improvement to be an arduous task. As a result, we are now beginning to see a number of trusts merging.

So many mergers are now taking place, most notably across the already highly academised regions, as the realisation that scale makes a difference is felt, particularly during what are difficult economic conditions.

NATIONAL POLITICS

We all know that the sectors of education and health are used as something of a political football. Everyone has been to school and has a view on education; not all of those views are based on our current reality, and few benefit from a wider, deeper more informed perspective. After 12 years of single-party politics, one might assume that we have been developing and evolving through a period of steady state where the rules remain consistent. However, with 12 secretaries of state in the last ten years and, famously, five in just over a year, it is ludicrous to suggest that the direction of educational policy has been consistent or clear.

The policy in relation to trusts has ebbed and flowed, beginning with a shift towards full academisation under the leadership of Nicky Morgan. Morgan, who was Secretary of State for Education between 2014 and 2016, set out her ambitions for schools in the 2016 white paper 'Educational Excellence Everywhere'. The paper declared that all schools would either be academies or be in the process of becoming an academy by 2020 and that local authorities would no longer be maintaining schools by the end of 2022. That ambition was abandoned within a matter of months.

Fast forward to 2022 and the DfE published another white paper with a similar (though somewhat diluted) goal: 'we want all schools to be in or joining a strong trust by 2030'.

To join a trust, a school must first become an academy. Yet this white paper stated that there was no legal requirement for schools to convert, and ministers introduced a new mechanism to help make the ambition a reality: for the first time, councils would be allowed to set up multi-academy trusts. Again, these plans were later scrapped; another example of changes of direction slowing the progress of the system. Despite this, the movement has continued to grow and there are no signs that this is slowing down. There is no suggestion yet from the opposition that the policy will dramatically change, and it would seem foolish to attempt to unpick the current system; it would take a long time and achieve little. As it stands, there appear to be three possible trajectories:

1. The movement is encouraged to grow, at which point there will inevitably be a tipping point and the need to be part of a family will become inevitable.

2. The system will not be encouraged, and we will end up with a hybrid akin to what we have now.

3. There will be a deliberate policy to move back to LA control, or another system of leadership, and governance will be introduced.

In March 2023, the Academies Regulatory and Commissioning Policy Paper outlined some key points and suggested that we are now in a phase where consolidating the best practice of the highest-performing trusts is critical. In doing so, the aspiration is to ensure better outcomes for children, provide better development for staff and, in turn, create a more resilient system. Who would not agree that these are laudable aspirations? The paper recognises the need for strong leadership which is supported and empowered. To do this, the DfE suggests that three things are important:

1. There needs to be a simple and proportionate regulatory strategy.

2. Better and more transparent commissioning decisions are required.

3. Sector expertise should be spread.

There is clearly a need to maintain choice for parents and a recognition that in certain areas, the dominance of one or a few trusts has made this impossible for some families. In recognising this, there is clearly a growing understanding that coherent geographical clustering is an important part of ensuring greater parental choice.

There continues to be a problem in terms of persistently under-performing schools, and the DfE recognises the need to develop high-quality trusts leading in every area and thereby supporting urgent school improvement. This understanding about what quality is and what metrics are used to define trust quality will be an important future consideration; how more of a regulatory approach (including what role Ofsted may play) will support this is not yet fully decided. In all of this, there is a recognition that times are tough, and obtaining value for money is increasingly important. Whatever the future holds, politicians are asking a lot from school leaders.

CHURCH/FAITH POLITICS

Looking to the future, we have to consider the role the church will play in our school system. The church authorities – Anglican and Catholic – clearly still have a significant role to play in this. There are so many small, rural church schools that need economies of scale and school improvement support, however their size makes them less attractive to any partner. How mixed MATs, national and regional clusters work in support of faith schools and authorities is not yet defined but needs resolving if the future is to be one of less division.

MIXED LANDSCAPE

Local authorities have taken very different views on academisation: some instructed all of their schools to find a home while others have actively discouraged the movement. As a result, the level of academisation varies significantly across the country as the diagram demonstrates. The variation between regions is startling with only 28% academisation in the North West as opposed to 62% in the South West. As the more academised regions evolve, the sustainability of the LA system becomes more fragile and the temptation to become part of the movement becomes more difficult to resist.

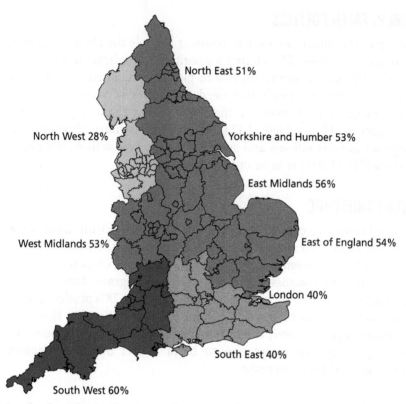

North East 51%

North West 28%

Yorkshire and Humber 53%

East Midlands 56%

West Midlands 53%

East of England 54%

London 40%

South East 40%

South West 60%

Levels of academisation across the country (source: Department for Education. Data available at: https://www.gov.uk/government/publications/open-academies-and-academy-projects-in-development (© Crown copyright 2014–2024)).

Many schools in regions with high numbers of academies have begun to recognise that the LA service is diminishing in both quality and scope and now also recognise that the option to form their own trust is less likely to be encouraged. Why is this the case? In part this is because in those regions of high academisation, the lack of intelligent design has meant that there is still a lot of sorting out to do. There is already an increase of mergers or takeovers where trusts, having grown to a certain point, perceive that they need to take over or be taken over if they are to achieve the necessary scale. Where high levels are embedded and while this rationalisation takes place, there is less and less space for new organisations to emerge. The horizon, therefore, must surely involve fewer trusts but with less variable outcomes or reputations.

SNOW (SCHOOLS NO ONE WANTS)

As we develop within the more academised regions, there is a danger that schools become isolated and increasingly less attractive for trusts. We all recognise that there are risks associated with every transfer but those risks are exacerbated by any of (or multiples of) the following criteria:

1. Size: The smaller the school, the less attractive it is for a trust. One-form-entry schools do not require half the work of a two-form-entry school.

2. Falling roll: To remain financially viable, schools need to be full, particularly when funding is tight.

3. Categories and difficult turnaround jobs: Clearly the scale of the school improvement challenge is something that needs to be considered before any transfer. Trusts must ensure that they have sufficient resources and this is increasingly difficult given the current funding pressures on schools.

4. Difficult HR issues: If the school has unresolved staffing difficulties (and they often have), any trust recognising this through due diligence will be concerned about the time and resources they will take to resolve.

5. Buildings: Schools that have been poorly served by their local authorities will often be in a poor state of repair. Significant capital investment may be needed to ensure that they are viable and a going concern.

2030–2040

If every school is to become part of a strong family of schools by 2030, then there is a lot to do and, in the doing, it would be helpful to have clearer political direction. There is, of course, a financial incentive to move towards academisation. Funding for schools has come under increasing pressure over recent years, despite government reassurances, with income not keeping in line with inflation or indeed energy rises. This alone is a powerful incentive for leaders to pool resources.

However, with the reserve positions of schools and trusts also diminishing, it is difficult to see a clear way forward for the system. Many of us working in health and education have called for a cross-party policy approach. For too long we have been reliant on gauging the varying political tides and following them in pursuit of working in the best interests of the children and families we serve. Trust leaders tend to consider the future in response to current politics and likely opportunities, leading to short-term planning. Institutions that have been around for a long time perhaps tend to think more strategically and have more of a long-term vision.

The general public, too, are confused; we regularly have to explain to parents the difference between an academy and a free school, how governance differs within a trust, and how both parties have encouraged changes to the system of running schools. The lack of equity across the system has evolved over decades with different levels of funding for different regions, different ways of managing SEND and inclusion, not to mention the differences in admissions. It has all become rather complicated and it would be wonderful to have a 10-year vision for education. It is a pipe dream of course, but not impossible.

It will never be easy to look towards the horizon when we are in the hands of party politics and the electoral cycle which provide the mist and fog that prevent us from seeing too far. As leaders, we need to remember that children joining reception classes in September 2024 will take A- and T-levels (or whatever examinations then exist) in the years approaching 2040 – that properly focuses horizon scanning.

ASIDE

Question for politicians and educational leaders

- Are leaders working towards a common goal or political vision for the future of education?

If the future is to be a more equitable one, prioritising the most disadvantaged schools and communities, we must make sure that the multi-school system is given resources that incentivise civic/balanced leadership. Are school leaders consistently working towards a common goal? I suggest not; I fear there are too many competing agendas. The most powerful, influential voices will define the horizon. If, locally, trusts are accountable only to their own outcomes then they are less likely to respond to their civic calling.

Perhaps it is time to hold trusts to account for area outcomes, encouraging collaboration between organisations.

INCLUSION

Perhaps the most important issue facing schools and school leaders at present is that of inclusion. There is no doubt that the pandemic has had a significantly negative impact on some of our most vulnerable children and families and the ripples of that continue to be felt. The enforced break from school has resulted in missed opportunities to diagnose SEND needs and it has also exacerbated some of the needs that children have, not least those with SEMH (social, emotional and mental health) challenges.

The degree to which children were affected by the loss of time in schools is still unclear but, as all school leaders will tell you, things feel different. There has clearly been a rise in SEMH issues presented within schools, attendance has dropped considerably and children are finding it much more difficult to stay in class. In-school truancy has become much more of a problem since the return to full-time education. We worked so hard to close the disadvantage gap over the last decade, with some significant success including for those children with SEND. The tragedy is that the gap has widened again post pandemic and it is likely to take some considerable time to make up that ground.

There are some pivotal questions and challenges for those of us leading within the multi-school system.

1. How is it that the funding for SEND is so variable across the country and how can the MAT system provide support? What needs to happen now?

It is really interesting to see how different local authorities manage funding. Those of us who run a trust across counties now recognise that there is not just one way of doing things and the responses differ surprisingly. Most EHCP (education, health and care plan) funding follows the child but not all; some authorities insist on a top-up system layering additional and unnecessary bureaucracy rather than supporting children and families directly. Working at scale brings fresh insights into the lack of consistency across political borders.

Why is there such a difference in the numbers of children with EHCPs across schools within the same area for example? The national average for EHCP is 1.8% per school, but within any local area you find that the numbers vary considerably. In part this is down to parental choice, but there are many examples where very popular and oversubscribed schools have low EHCP numbers and the multi-school movement has highlighted this lack of equity. Some LAs are responding to this directly, coordinating a joint response across the LA to best meet the needs of the children and to spread the load fairly. Many are not and simply do not have the capacity or intention to do so fearing, perhaps, a backlash from parents.

As trust leaders, we have a responsibility to suggest new and improved ways of responding to the demand, working collaboratively with multiple partners. As the system matures, this becomes more and more important. If we are going to work at scale, and if local authorities are going to retain responsibility for SEND, then we need to consider how this works in practice. The LA SEND response is currently designed around a single-school system. Ultimately, the LA holds the purse strings and schools and trusts rightly acknowledge the key role they play.

2. How much of an impact did the pandemic have on our children and how are we going to meet the challenges over the coming years? How can the MAT system support this?

We know that the system is struggling to meet the demand: there is a national shortage of support and expertise. Try getting additional support from mental health professionals, for anxiety, depression, eating disorders or self harm. The CAMHS (child and adolescent mental health services) system is overloaded and the burden sits with schools and parents who are ill equipped to deal with such complex needs. The advantages of working at scale must in some way support a response to this crisis and that is something we are all wrestling with.

In the first instance, the opportunity for SENDcos (special educational needs and disabilities coordinators) and LSAs (learning support assistants) to come together is an immediate advantage. Being a SENDco is a lonely job and very stressful. The ability to at least share some of this burden with colleagues in a similar role should not be underestimated. The opportunity to disseminate best practice and to co-create some shared solutions and responses is much needed but it is obvious that an increasing number of children are not thriving in mainstream schools. Those teachers who invited the most vulnerable children into schools during the recent industrial action noticed how much happier many of these children appeared when working in a smaller setting away from the noise, conflict and general hubbub of normal school life.

The opportunity, then, for trust leaders to work within the system and set up specialist and alternative provision is obvious – but a word of caution: specialist provision is, as it says, specialised! Those responsible for leading mainstream schools should not imagine that they can suddenly turn their hand to specialist settings. We must surely use the knowledge within the system to work in partnership. How this can best be achieved is not yet clear though there are some green shoots with emerging partnerships between local authorities, trusts and special schools.

3. How are we going to recruit and train colleagues to support the system given the challenges of funding and pay? What support do we need to give to staff to ensure that we retain them?

We recognise that support assistants can earn more money working in the local supermarket or coffee franchise. How, then, do we ensure that the right people can be encouraged to work with our most vulnerable children and families? More than that, how do we ensure that they can be encouraged to stay within the system?

The average tenure is short and the stresses are often difficult to manage. It takes a very special person to work effectively with our most vulnerable children. They are unfailingly positive, patient and kind, possessing considerable inter- and intra-personal intelligence. They are often well qualified and have considerable life experience. It is a vocation, but in return we must ensure that they are thanked, praised and remunerated appropriately. Too often they are taken for granted and current financial pressures make it impossible to pay what the job deserves.

All too frequently our precious resources are underused. In part this is because support and teaching colleagues are unable to find the time to plan or discuss the best approaches in the classroom. How often do we visit classrooms and notice that there does not appear to be a plan between teacher and support assistant? Finding time for them is vital, to ensure that these key professionals coordinate their work delivering the curriculum to meet the needs of all children. In relying on supply LSAs, we simply pass on taxpayers' money to unregulated agencies and receive much poorer service. There must be a better way to deploy resources.

4.   What is the structure within the school system that will best support inclusion?

There is considerable debate about school exclusions and there is also considerable pressure to deal with deteriorating behaviour across schools, particularly post pandemic. We all recognise that children from disadvantaged backgrounds, those with additional learning needs and those from ethnically diverse backgrounds are much more likely to be excluded from school. When they are excluded, we consider other placements and options which often do not meet their needs and can be very expensive. The system we have is not working, and the profession must work together with all partners to resolve this chronic situation.

Children with SEND are too often excluded because we fail to meet their needs. In part this is because we do not have sufficient resources but it is also because we do not have sufficient expertise and are not efficient in our use of resources. Research from the Education Endowment Foundation is clear that 'quality first teaching' is the most effective mechanism to improve SEND provision. The most important investment, therefore, is in professional development, refining classroom practice to better meet the needs of children.

Too often, children with an EHCP, and for whom specialist provision is specified within that plan, do not have an appropriate education. There are simply not enough places available and these children end up in some form of alternative provision which simply does not meet their needs.

We all recognise the high-stakes nature of behaviour challenges, and that children are let down when behaviour systems are unable to flex and adapt to meet their needs. Children with SEND often move from exclusion to negotiated transfers to permanent exclusion and then into alternative provision. None of this deals with the issue. Parents, too, bear some responsibility for choosing the appropriate provision. They often have a desire for their children to remain in mainstream settings when a special school might be the most appropriate place. Too often the relationship between school and parents breaks down, with parents understandably being the principal advocate for their child and schools recognising the disproportionate impact children can have on staff and other children.

Trusts have an opportunity to improve things by developing their own alternative and special-school provision. This is already happening and where it is, we must make sure that this provision is shared and intelligently designed.

ASIDE

Questions for trust leaders

- In recreating the school system, how can we ensure that the needs of children and families with SEND are met, developing better structures, systems and processes to create a more inclusive environment?

- Will trusts move to opening their own special schools and resource bases to meet needs? Shall we see more mergers between special-school trusts and mainstream-school trusts?

We have a wonderful opportunity to work in partnership: a partnership between trusts, the DfE and local authorities to carefully consider the provision required for inclusion. The system urgently needs to ensure that there are sufficient special-school places and consider how mainstream schools might further support inclusion, providing some specialist settings.

JOBS

THE LEADER

As start-ups in any context emerge, the need to remodel and reconsider the roles within the organisation becomes apparent.

Often trusts have begun from single schools where the founding CEO has been the headteacher of the founding school. Where this is the case, trusts may begin slowly, growing school by school. This can be painful and time consuming.

The emerging CEO often has to juggle three jobs:

- retaining some leadership function within the original school
- considering how to support schools joining the organisation, encouraging collaboration and fulfilling the executive principal brief
- carrying out the CEO function; establishing the vision and values and the growth strategy, and developing partnerships.

A key step is to identify the best roles to establish to give the best possible start to the organisation. Inevitably, as scale is not yet there, employees often have to carry out more than one role.

In his book *Being the CEO*, Michael Pain[5] lists six dimensions of the role:

1. Translating the vision into a compelling narrative.
2. Building an open, transparent and constructive relationship with the board.
3. Being the chief talent officer and culture maker.

---

5   Pain, M. (2019) *Being the CEO: The Six Dimensions of Organisational Leadership.* Woodbridge, John Catt.

4. Enabling improvement and innovation as an 'organisational habit'.

5. Securing organisational sustainability and compliance.

6. Fostering key relationships, building social and professional capital.

The difference between executive school leadership and headship is something that needs to be well considered by the emerging trust board.

When two or more schools come together to form a trust, the decision on who leads must be made – and this can get in the way of intelligent design. There is no doubt that ego can obstruct sensible decision making, as can local politics. The question of who is in charge is rarely about who is best to be in charge, and who is best to be in charge is not an easy question. The truth is that the qualities required for successful headship are not necessarily those most needed for executive headship; it is a very different role. The move to becoming the CEO is a similarly large step, and the requisite skill set is just not the same. There is a similar challenge with mergers, and trustees must wrestle with the question: What are the qualities required for a successful CEO within the multi-school system?

The following questions need to be addressed, both by potential CEOs and by the boards that appoint them.

- Is the executive leader able to get off the dance floor and lead from the balcony, enabling others to lead, facilitating and encouraging and interfering only when necessary?
- Does the executive leader possess entrepreneurial skills, taking appropriate risks and coming up with innovative ideas and strategies?
- Is the executive able to network and develop relationships that further the organisation? Are they able to see beyond their own working environment to make connections that will feed the trust into the future?
- Is the executive able to flex leadership styles and preferences to adapt to different situations?
- Is the executive politically savvy, and do they understand the motivations and interests of others and attempt to negotiate and compromise?
- Can they read a room and respond appropriately?

- Do they understand the needs of the whole system and are they prepared to adjust their aspirations to benefit the sector?
- Are they able to let go of single-school improvement, going slower to go further? Some headteachers are not yet ready to consider multi-school work, recognising that the convoy must move forward together leaving no school behind.

THE EXECUTIVE TEAM

Critical to the success of any organisation is the effectiveness of the central team. Typically this includes finance, HR, ICT and school improvement. As the organisation evolves, these key members create the confidence that the organisation can work at scale. During the start-up phase, the central team is also key in ensuring compliance, encouraging innovation and developing strong relationships with the board.

There is an intimacy during the start-up phase; something we also see when building new schools. In the free school movement, the pioneering staff in the first year or two work so closely together, and develop relationships that would not normally happen in a fully established school. Early career teachers and middle leaders find themselves working very closely with the senior team.

As the school grows, this becomes unsustainable. The relationships naturally settle into a more traditional hierarchy and those used to having the ear of the headteacher have to accept that it is not always going to be possible. Similarly, the headteacher can become disconnected from the staff with whom they may have previously had a close relationship. The same thing can happen within a trust central team, often resulting initially in a rather flat leadership structure. As the organisation develops, this can become problematic; there is often no obvious number two in the structure and as the trust grows, the team is forced to reform. At this point, careful thought has to go into what that structure looks like.

SCHOOL IMPROVEMENT ROLES

One essential consideration is the structure of the school improvement function and what this might consist of. In its infancy, the structure tends to use the most effective school practitioners from within the founding school or schools. Often called 'lead practitioners', these highly skilled subject colleagues are asked to work in other schools that need additional support. This can take the form of individual subject leads but it might also include areas such as assessment, safeguarding, inclusion or curriculum planning. There are advantages in deploying staff across schools, of course, and they are often highly valued and respected. However, there are limitations and risks:

- Where the most influential staff are dragged into school improvement across the organisation, this can cause some resentment. There are early indications that the founding schools become the least positive members of the growing family, with a feeling that they are constantly 'capacity givers' rather than 'improvement receivers'. These schools may feel that they are losing some of their best staff.

- These roles tend to be part time and fixed term. As a result, colleagues complain that they do not have the time or resources to make a sufficient impact. There is a limit to what people can achieve when the role is not their main job!

- Hierarchy is an issue. Staff visiting other schools do not always have the authority to make lasting changes and their initiatives can be thwarted by internal leaders jealously guarding their areas of responsibility.

- It can be difficult to ensure clarity of purpose; if you are not careful, school improvement functions can lack coordination, with different colleagues prioritising certain areas. Deciding who is in charge of school improvement at scale is vital.

EDUCATION LEADS (EXECUTIVE PRINCIPALS)

Many established trusts have restructured a number of times, learning from their mistakes. The executive roles are an important part of the considerations which underpin effective dissemination. Many begin with an executive primary and an executive secondary role.

The need for wider collaboration has been discussed in previous chapters. Again, however, it is surprising how trusts facilitate this differently with a number of models and the different size-related constraints and opportunities. Most mature trusts operate a structure that includes executive phase leaders, often primary or secondary executives. Many of the larger trusts add the director of education role that may or may not become the deputy CEO.

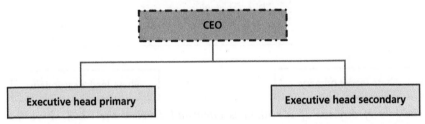

In some hierarchical structures, the executive phase leaders come directly below the CEO.

The decision to have a director of education as a number two avoids the risk of developing too flat a structure but can only be achieved at scale. In contrast, a number of trusts have gone down a more operational route appointing a COO as the trust's deputy.

As the trust develops, there is a danger, particularly where strong leadership is established in both phases, that the improvement work becomes disjointed and lacking coordination. Often the phases move apart and have little to do with each other. As a result, many mixed-phase trusts have moved more quickly to appoint a 'director of education' who sits above the executive leads and ensures that the curriculum and school improvement work is coordinated. There is no right or wrong way but nor is there yet any empirical evidence about what might be the most effective way to structure trusts.

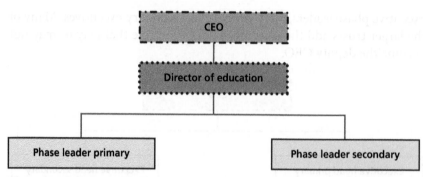

The role of director of education is often added below the CEO, above the executive leads.

All of this needs to be considered upon inception.

INTERNAL EVOLUTION

As a trust develops, so too must its structures, systems and processes. Evolving from a start-up cottage industry into a mature organisation is not an easy transition and requires ambitious and proactive decision-making and thinking. The structural differences between small-, medium- and large trusts are enormous and it is, of course, helpful to consider where the organisation is headed before you begin. The Tuckman (1969) model of team development still resonates, with trusts having to 'reform' or adjourn frequently.

The Tuckman model of team development (1969)

There are clearly some tipping points here that most will recognise. Beyond a certain size, the need for certain roles becomes acute. At what point will we not be able to survive without an estates manager, a safeguarding lead and a data processor, for example? Systems that worked when they involved a few schools are found wanting at scale and human error becomes more common.

The key role of the executive leader is, again, one that headteachers may not be prepared for, particularly if they have not yet worked within a trust. The move from single-school improvement to school improvement at scale is a significant one. At the heart of this work is the curriculum which can underpin school improvement work at scale. The role of the executive lead therefore involves garnering collaboration, predicated by conversations about pedagogy, curriculum and assessment. There is an inherent tension here that needs to be overcome with political sophistication and professional credibility. Executive leads need to be educational leads, first and foremost, if the organisation is to move forward prioritising teaching and leadership.

Headteachers and governing bodies understand the value of an effective senior leadership team; well-formed and dynamic teams transform schools. We all know that. Able headteachers cannot do it on their own. The same is true for families of schools and there are two other leadership groups to consider. As trusts develop, the headteacher group – primary or secondary or combined – becomes an important force; the same is true of the central team leadership structure. Ensuring that leaders undertake tasks that are right for their school but also for the trust is a key consideration.

MISSION CREEP

Inevitably, newly created roles have a habit of moving beyond their original boundaries or job descriptions and for often positive reasons. For example, leaders who are originally asked to lead on curriculum collaboration at KS3 begin to work across phases; a primary inclusion lead begins to look at transition and involves the leaders in the secondary phase. It is all laudable and somewhat inevitable. As trusts develop, it can be difficult to tie down job descriptions and this can lead to some resentment. Another gremlin to be grappled!

ASIDE

Questions for leaders

As roles develop and the mindset begins to shift from independence to interdependence, it is worth considering again:

- What roles are needed within the organisation to best facilitate school improvement and effective collaboration?
- How do these roles change, develop and adapt over time?

How often do we really consider the skill set required for a particular job at a particular time? Different leadership approaches are required within trusts at different phases of their development. One of the greatest advantages of a trust is the ability to retain talented staff who have the potential to make a difference across schools. To do so, leaders have to look strategically at staffing structures and individuals, considering who has the potential to lead at scale.

Being a trust leader requires an acceptance that losing a valued member of staff to a trust-wide role is a good thing. And, requirements change over time, leading to the need to refresh and rethink.

KNOWLEDGE

Within the new system and associated structures, we are constantly reflecting to ensure that we seek out knowledge in order to make sensible decisions about the future development of our organisations. Some of this can be found, of course, in the existing knowledge and rich evidence base of established businesses and companies. There is a wealth of resources on offer for those within education who are interested in furthering their understanding of executive leadership; trusts are effectively companies which need to be well led and governed.

Trust-leadership learning is less-well documented than leadership in the business sector: founding CEOs have set up their organisations differently. One CEO involved in a merger combining two medium-sized trusts into one large trust comprising 13,000 children and 28 schools recently shared her experience with me: 'You would imagine that these similar-sized trusts might have been set up in approximately the same way but the truth is that they are entirely different.' An understanding about how these organisations have been set up becomes obvious through a merger.

Our organisation recently took part in a review involving three other local trusts facilitated by Challenge Partners,[6] an organisation set up to support schools and trusts to reflect through a different lens using peers from other organisations to do so. There are effectively six sections supporting this reflection.

1. Context and relevant information about the trust

---

6   Challenge Partners, six sections supporting reflection, reproduced with permission.

2. What the trust is trying to achieve: its vision, values, ethos and culture and the extent to which academies understand and reflect these

3. The impact of the trust on the quality of education, curriculum and pedagogy

4. The trust's approach to multi-school improvement

5. The MAT factor: how the trust knows and demonstrates its impact on the improvement of its academies and outcomes for students including disadvantaged learners and students with SEND

6. Capacity and sustainability of the trust to improve its schools

The last four of the above sections are, of course, critical and are the ones that are bespoke to school improvement at scale; that is the knowledge base which is less well known or understood. In understanding how we support school improvement, there are some further, deeper, challenging questions:

Are the roles and responsibilities of the trust and schools for school improvement known and clear to all? To what extent is school improvement trust or school led?

At the heart of this again lies culture: some trusts have evolved for good reason via a standardised route and there is a top-down hierarchical approach to school improvement. For others, there are higher levels of autonomy, and co-constructed collaborative school improvement is different from the more 'command and control' approach. The extent to which school improvement activities are carried out 'with' or 'to' is a good test of the culture of the organisation.

Who should lead/drive multi-school improvement? What are the various roles and how effective are they?

It is important to consider what roles provide the biggest impact, as we discussed in the previous chapter. From middle-leader practitioner roles to executive functions, we need to consider at what point in the evolution of the organisation these roles become more relevant or less relevant. As yet, there is little shared knowledge about what the most effective structures might be and at what point they might be more or less relevant.

How does the trust know the strengths and weaknesses of its schools? Who checks school improvement?

This quality assurance question is an important one. Some trusts have external SIPs (school improvement partners). Some use score cards highlighting very publicly the relative strengths and weaknesses of each school. Most trusts have developed a cycle of quality assurance leading to school development plans but this is different across the sector, again some co-constructed and some more top-down driven.

How does the trust challenge all schools to improve? Are there well-established, robust QA and self-evaluation systems and processes in place to diagnose what needs to improve?

It is essential to consider whether schools are moving forwards or backwards; early diagnosis of a negative trend can be the defining factor in when and how to intervene. I would argue that there is no such thing as a 'stuck school'; schools either move forwards or backwards, the challenge is to spot early movements in the wrong direction. Where school improvement activity works well, executive staff or central team school improvement staff are in agreement with school middle and senior leaders about the relevant strengths and weaknesses and what needs to be done.

Consensus is not always achieved: on many occasions, working either as a school improvement advisor or within our trust schools, there has been a disagreement about what we see. Accurate diagnosis of what needs to improve and how to improve it are at the heart of good trust work. Where school improvement activities are ineffective, leaders collude and reassure each other that things are well when they are clearly not. The culture of high challenge, disagreeing well, being reflective and adaptive, is not always what we see in schools. Egos get in the way and school and trust leaders can respond to the high accountability nature of the system by reverting to self-protectionist behaviours.

How do we identify and share exemplary practice and knowledge across the trust?

This is perhaps the most important question and leads to a further question: in sharing, how do we make sure that we don't dilute the school improvement pool, robbing Peter to pay Paul? The answer for many lies in the investment of curriculum- and pedagogy-related collaboration groups, in action-research initiatives, in school visits. To make improvements, professionals must be given the space, time and encouragement to collaborate so that worthwhile dissemination can take place.

Research about the impact of collaboration goes back many years. Historically, the role of a teacher or school leader was an isolated one, but the micro-political perspective of schools has changed over time. The term 'reflective practitioner' first made its way into the lexicon of school leadership in the 1980s (Kolb, 1984) and early 1990s (Schön, 1991). This reflection, when done with others, leads to collaboration and joint learning.

The shift towards reflective practice, collaboration and dissemination is at the heart of the multi-school movement in pursuit of interdependence. Our challenge is to ensure that knowledge is shared. The inevitable question about what happens to the individual's integrity and autonomy in a constantly collaborative structure and culture is something we are all wrestling with. Some argue that there can be a respect for individualism, but not individuality. The larger the school, the more difficult it is to embed collaborative structures; it is even more difficult to achieve this across schools! Providing the conditions for effective collaboration, while also making the parameters clear, is essential. I hear the word collaboration mentioned often, but what it means in different trusts varies considerably and not all are managing to share knowledge and learning across schools effectively.

What management systems are in place for collecting and reviewing core data that gives insights into performance, and a range of other areas useful to the trust? How effective are they?

Providing live and meaningful data to the board and to school leadership teams, which usefully compares schools and gives rise to the most important questions, is the aim. Often the collection of data is unwieldy and time consuming; by the time we interrogate the data, much of it have become largely redundant. Yet this knowledge is vital to spot the trends of decline or improvement, ensuring we have support systems and, critically, staff that can lead effectively.

Is there clarity for academy leaders about what is provided by the trust centrally and what academies are expected to pay for, regarding improvement support?

For some, the support comes simply in the form of quality assurance; for others, the support is deeper, with leaders working in school, helpfully blurring the lines of school/trust. This is one of the most common areas for misunderstanding. Being clear about what schools get from central services is a key part of due diligence but also something to be interrogated by headteachers and governors throughout each academic year.

What is the quality of the support and how do you know the impact?

Much has been said about the way in which we externally quality assure our trusts. The truth is we do not do this in any coordinated way, yet. In the event that multiple schools within the trusts fall into categories, or are noted to be significantly under-performing, agencies such as the DfE or Ofsted can take a closer look. At this point, however, it is arguably too late. It can take considerable time and resources to turn around schools and trusts; the decision about the viability of trusts, about whether re-brokering might be appropriate, takes time. Meanwhile, children in these schools with only one chance of an education lose out!

Much is also always said about the pressure on headteachers, particularly in relation to inspection, a pressure shared across a family of schools. Of course, schools within trusts will only be successful if they are in receipt of quality school-improvement work led by effective central teams. Ofsted can inspect several schools within a trust, effectively reviewing that support, that curriculum model several times. It would be more helpful if they were to review the trust school-improvement work one time, releasing some of the pressure on an overburdened system.

Surely this will be the evolution of the quality assurance process across our system: it is time for the framework to take its next evolutionary step. Politicians seem to be anxious still that parents retain some information about the quality of education via an outdated and misunderstood grading system underpinned by bland reports and single-word judgements that tell us very little about the school. Our knowledge of trusts is not yet consistent and fully evidence based. It should be!

What is the relationship between trust governance and local governing bodies, advisory bodies or committees, in terms of their accountability for school improvement and student outcomes?

Many trusts have moved away from local governance of schools, particularly where it relates to school improvement, though there are good examples of where this function can still lie with local boards. It is important that the challenge of school improvement is led by the main board and supported externally, avoiding the echo chamber of internal central teams. In addition, recruiting educational experts onto boards is critical – although not easy. The ability for board members and local governors to visit schools and to observe or take part in school-improvement activities remains vitally important.

Can the trust provide examples of where leaders have engaged with external organisations or individuals to bring about significant school improvement?

Again, we have to be careful that we avoid the echo-chamber effect, particularly in larger trusts. The need to ensure that internal best practice is disseminated remains critical, but it is also important to make sure we are looking outside of the organisation to find local, regional and national best practice to learn from.

As far back as 2015, the South-West division in partnership with ISOS published its own Trust Capacity Framework split into six sections, and trusts were encouraged to RAG (red, amber, green) rate their organisations alongside some helpful criteria. One of the difficulties here was that many of the criteria references implied a particular view on standardisation. In other words, a green rating was given in an area that had moved across the continuum to a more standardised position.

Vision, culture and ethos	People and partners	Teaching and learning	Curriculum and assessment	Quality assurance and accountability	Governance capability
• Clarity of purpose • Understanding of needs • Leading a culture of improvement	• Building capacity for improvement • Recruiting, developing and retaining talent	• Approach to pedagogy • Leadership of teaching • Evidence-based professional learning models	• Curriculum, principles, intent and alignment • Intentional use of assessment	• Knowing schools quantitatively • Knowing schools qualitatively	• Governance structures and skills • Capability to refresh and renew

The six sections of the Trust Capacity Framework (source: Trust Capacity Framework – now MAT Assurance Framework – developed by ISOS Partnership for the Department for Education © Crown Copyright).

In April 2023, the DfE published its *Trust Quality Descriptions*.[7] This has been a long time coming, yet worth the wait: a strong example of practice shaping policy. This framework is split into five sections:

1. High-quality and inclusive education: culture; curriculum; outcomes; accessible to all; inclusive pastoral support; enrichment; behaviour and attendance; destination; collaboration

2. School improvement: culture; school improvement model; transformation; system-led improvement

3. Workforce: culture, workload, retention; environment; developing early career teachers; CPD; collaboration, line-management and career progression; equality, diversity and inclusion

4. Finance and operations: culture; financial strategy; resource allocation; capital strategy; reserves; financial information management

5. Governance and leadership: challenge, support, quality assurance and partnerships

We are deepening our understanding and knowledge base about trusts: how they are structured, how they work and whether or not they are effective. As we do so, there is a need to share that learning so that we recognise what works and what does not. The Confederation of School Trusts in partnership with the Ambition Institute released an assurance framework in 2023 which builds on the DfE quality descriptions.[8]

---

7 Department for Education (2023). *Trust Quality Descriptions*. Available at: https://assets.publishing.service.gov.uk/media/64a68ab94dd8b3000f7fa566/ Annex_A_-_Trust_Quality_Descriptions_July_2023_.pdf (© Crown copyright 2023).

8 Confederation of School Trusts (2023). *Building strong trusts: assurance framework*. Available at: https://cstuk.org.uk/knowledge/guidance-and-policy/building-strong-trusts-assurance-framework

ASIDE

Question

- Is it not time to change and coordinate the quality assurance system?

We could continue to inspect single-academy trusts or LA schools but combine this with whole-scale inspection of trusts. If MAT inspections looked in detail at 3–5 schools within the framework (a deep-dive system for schools rather than subjects), could we not save significant sums of money and valuable resources? Effective trusts know their schools well; this needs to be checked but you don't need to check every single school to do this!

LEADERSHIP

Specifically trust leadership, because it is different!

Many of us found in the early years of becoming a trust that the phrase 'The Trust' became common parlance; heard often and not always in complimentary terms. Initially, I didn't notice it but increasingly I became bothered by what was meant, and began to ask people. Of course, it turns out, it referred to the central team – to the executives, to the board – often anonymous to teachers in schools. It might seem insignificant but this label highlights the paradigm shift that is important for all trusts, trust leaders and employees.

We have all heard the story of the cleaner working at NASA who, when asked what she did, said, 'I am helping put a man on the Moon'. This collective thinking, understanding and doing is fundamental. The question, 'why do we exist?' was clearly understood by all employees at NASA but it is not yet well enough defined in many trusts. When staff refer to 'the trust', they are implying that there is somehow another organisation, at odds with their own. The people using the term 'the trust' *are* the trust, but are yet to acknowledge it or understand fully what that means.

If the system is predicated on collaboration, dissemination and cooperation, then the words we use and the way we act become really important. Where culture is unhealthy, we hear words like *they, them* and, that phrase again, 'the trust'. Where it is healthy, people commonly use words like *us* and *our*. In order to highlight the issue, some trusts have begun to ask people specifically to use the term 'central team' rather than 'the trust'. Many have adopted the phrase 'school is trust, trust is school'. This collective thinking is hard to achieve; schools are busy places and the pressures are acute. Having to think more widely about the impact things will have on other schools is an additional burden on busy teachers and leaders.

Once the mission purpose and values are properly defined, understood and enacted, this can help to support collective endeavour. Effective trust leadership can require different behaviours to effective general school leadership. I recognise that there are a lot of questions in this book, not all of them answered effectively, but here are two more that we will attempt to answer within this chapter:

1. What do we mean by an effective trust leader?
2. What does it mean to be an effective trust leader within your organisation?

At a time where recruitment and retention are difficult, these issues commonly come to light via poaching! We find that as staff get to know other schools and other staff they might, and have been known to, informally approach members of staff to encourage them to apply for vacancies as they arise, particularly for difficult-to-fill posts. These direct approaches, often without any conversations with other leaders or headteachers, undermine the spirit of the trust and are damaging to trust leaderships.

Trust takes time to build and consensus can be difficult to reach. On occasion, some schools might have to slow down or change direction in order for all schools to move forward together. This is a difficult leadership concept to grasp and is not always popular with ambitious and talented school leaders determined to move things forward apace in their own schools. This point speaks to the long-term ambitions of schools: architects versus surgeons. We are reminded again of the proverb, 'if you want to go fast go alone, if you want to go far go together'. Trusts exist to improve schools; all schools, moving forward together. It is simply not acceptable that we can allow some schools to make rapid improvement while others decline.

Clearly there will be a degree of 'in-trust' variation, where some schools make more rapid improvement, but if we get it right then collaboration, dissemination and the resulting alignment should ensure that all within the family can improve. To do so, decisions must be taken at the executive level and we will not please all the leaders all the time. Trusts, where phases have moved at different paces and in different directions (primary moving away from secondary, for example), have often later regretted it, having to work hard to realign systems, practices and philosophies.

The more layers we build into the system, the more difficult communication becomes. Adding layers of roles – central teams, executive leaders, curriculum leads, collaboration groups etc. – makes the job of communication more and more difficult and there is the ever-present danger that leaders will move in a direction not considered or agreed centrally. Herein lies the great tension of multi-school work. Many of us recognise that creativity is vital for an organisation to flourish; we want to encourage independence of thought, want the entrepreneurs to be entrepreneurial, want the divergent thinkers to challenge the way and to support us to change direction when we should. The more we work together, the more we disseminate; the more we all begin to do things in a similar way, creativity is stifled and we become less agile. If we are going to encourage innovation, we have to be clear about where and when we might expect it; we have to be alert and reflective, willing to adapt in response to divergent thinking. Otherwise, we risk going stale; losing the edge and the capacity to adapt quickly.

Effective trust leadership requires thoughtful consideration about where schools and school leaders have autonomy and where they do not, and this changes as the trust develops. If we are to understand what trust leadership looks like in our organisation, we have to be clear. One useful way to consider this is a simple three-column exercise, using a very broad framework which might look something like the following table:

Leadership	Aligned	Under discussion (tension)	Freedom/ autonomy
Curriculum			
Pedagogy			
Safeguarding			
Behaviour/systems			
Assessment			
Etc.			

Clearly how it is ordered, how many columns and what we call the columns is trust dependent but the idea is simple and important. Leaders need to have clear direction, and need to be constantly reminded if we are to be reassured that our expectations for trust leadership are understood.

BESPOKE TRUST LEADERSHIP: WHAT IS EFFECTIVE LEADERSHIP WITHIN YOUR TRUST?

To answer this question, let's look at Lencioni's six suggestions. Lencioni suggests that when creating a healthy organisation, the second discipline is about ensuring that there is clarity.

1. Why do we exist? (Why do we make a difference in the world?)
2. How do we behave? (One, two or three absolute musts in terms of behaviour.)
3. What do we do? (An organisation has to know what business it is in.)
4. How will we succeed? (How will we make intentional decisions that will set us apart?)
5. What is most important right now? (Every organisation needs a rallying cry.)
6. Who must do what? (Do we really understand the roles and responsibilities of the team?)

The second question, 'How do we behave?', is vital to ask when we are considering how we lead and this is something that (in my trust) we have spent a good deal of time on, developing three core words to describe how we might encourage everyone to behave: *reflective, collaborative, creative.*

The *reflection* element requires us to doubt ourselves; to be critical, candid and thoughtful. It sounds obvious but so many schools and school leaders see things the way they want to see them, particularly when times are tough. The high-stakes accountability culture that pervades the system makes it hard to look in the mirror, particularly when we feel things are getting away from us. The formal inspection framework is essentially challenge built on power. Inspectors have the authority to make evaluations and issue challenges, and it is very difficult indeed for headteachers and teachers even to question, let alone reject, such evaluations and challenges. The need to engage in uncomfortable external and internal quality assurance is obvious. So too is the need for challenging professional development conversations underpinned, where possible, by a positive coaching culture.

If the culture is right then trust leaders, headteachers and teachers can challenge each other without the dramatic consequences of inspection, producing a much-less-defensive response. If colleagues at all levels can be encouraged to be reflective and responsive to that reflection, then the culture of school improvement is solid.

The word *collaboration* asks that leaders are committed to dissemination and the resulting compromises that might be required. In order for collaboration to be effective, we have to commit time, resources and energy. Of course, the more energy we commit to dissemination, the more likely it is that systems, processes and practice will tend to align. Alignment is the inevitable consequence of collaboration and dissemination but hopefully not at the expense of *creativity*. It all makes the last of the three verbs the most challenging. Of course you have to give the time and space to collaborate effectively, and in a busy school environment this is hard. Those that don't provide the right conditions for collaboration don't move forward together.

It is all very well saying that we are going to encourage creativity, but if dissemination results in stifling it, then we have surely failed. How then do we supply the conditions for encouraging creativity while being true to the principles of dissemination? The three-column exercise above is an attempt to ensure that leaders understand their creative freedoms but it instinctively feels restrictive from the outset.

The last four questions, relating to how an organisation defines success, are nuanced: if the overarching mission is 'To tackle disadvantage in ...', then the success of the most vulnerable students will be key. If the vision is to ensure that the 'whole child' is developed, then the metrics of success might not just be examination outcomes, value added or otherwise. Where trusts are strong, everyone understands what the metrics of success are and they are shared across the family of schools.

Discovering what is important now can be a useful way to align leaders' thinking. Involving multiple strands of leaders across schools within the quality assurance process is a useful way to ensure that trust-wide leadership, reflection and thinking are encouraged. We cannot expect our leaders to lead across a family of schools if they have little or no experience across our schools. Once we have agreed on what is important now, then we can agree on who does what.

It is important for us to be clear about what we hold dear, how we expect people to behave and the sort of trust leadership that we require within our organisation. We cannot expect new recruits to know all about us simply from the interview process, so it is important to consider how we show up, how we talk about ourselves through the recruitment process. Trusts come in all shapes and sizes and with very different ideological approaches. Less-mature trusts often find this difficult, having not yet fully realised who they are or what they aspire to be. As a result, people can accept positions without fully understanding what type of organisation they are joining.

ASIDE

Questions for leaders

- Have trust leaders considered what appropriate leadership behaviours are within this organisation?
- Is the organisation clear about what creative and effective leadership looks like here?

Finding out how people think is an essential part of the recruitment process. If we recruit people into the multi-school movement who do not buy into or yet fully understand the philosophy of collaboration and 'trust leadership', we are making a big mistake. It is really important to ensure that the evolving paradigm shift in trust thinking is built into training and development programmes.

MISTAKES

If the system is going to thrive and survive, if CEOs are going to support the system to improve further, then we should acknowledge the mistakes we have made, learn from them and improve as a result. In the spirit of reflective leadership, let's look at some of what has gone wrong and what needs to improve.

What right do we have to be critical when we have all made mistakes and continue to make them? It is better that we own them and try to share our learning and reflections.

POLITICS AND QUALITY ASSURANCE

In early 2012, the then education secretary, Michael Gove[9], said:

> Why is this particularly important? Because it flies in the face of those critics who say that what we are advocating is a narrow, one-size-fits-all, Gradgrindian model. Critics who seek to set up false binary divides between rigour and creativity; between excellence and well-being; between an outstanding academic education and one which concentrates on character. Fryer's[10] work shows us that certain characteristics are related to high achievement with a variety of educational approaches. Expect excellence; offer intensive support; spend time in the classroom;

---

9   Gove, M. (2012). Available at: https://www.gov.uk/government/speeches/michael-gove-speech-on-academies (© Crown Copyright 2012).

10 Fryer is an economics professor at Harvard University. He researches economic theory, empirical evidence and randomised experiments to help inform government policies. He has been quoted widely in relation to his work on education, inequality and race.

use accountability intelligently; champion achievement... These are the principles that underpin great schools.

That's why while academies come in different shapes and sizes, and while academy heads come from a variety of different educational traditions, and while the Academy programme is explicitly designed to let a thousand – or rather 1529 – flowers bloom, it's nonetheless clear that the best academies share common characteristics. These are the characteristics clearly reflected in Fryer's findings. These are the things we are advocating. And to say somehow this equates to demanding a return to the Victorian era is more than a lazy pastiche – it's downright disingenuous.

This reference to 1529 flowers is interesting. Ten years on, far more flowers have bloomed but this horticultural metaphor and subsequent policy inevitably gave rise to flowers blooming in places where we least expected, where the flowers were not sustainable and where the ground conditions were not conducive to a healthy garden. In short, some flowers have withered or died! This rather serendipitous approach to 'growing' the sector has left us with legacy issues. Not all trusts are sustainable, not all have grown sensibly, not all have supported schools as effectively as they should.

Perhaps Michael Gove gave the system the best long-term chance of success. If the system had not been allowed to flourish and grow as quickly as it has, then there was a danger that it may have faltered. Politicians may have decided to row back or change direction again. As it was, the decision to give the entrepreneurial and competitive instinct the opportunity to flourish meant that the current of academisation became strong and irresistible. It gave rise to rapid growth and, sometimes, poor design. It does mean that we will be sorting it out for some time to come.

There have been mistakes in the free-market approach that resulted in rapid expansion and a less-than-intelligent design. This, combined with the variation of response from a number of stakeholders, has generated an over-complicated and highly variable system that requires some unpicking and, where appropriate, re-brokering. To do this, we will need to have greater powers of intervention and external quality assurance.

The Regulatory and Commissioning policy paper (2023) does accept some of the current issues and acknowledges many of the current frustrations. In addition, it suggests that the failures have been 'rare' but also 'impactful'.

And now turning to the internal issues, those mistakes made by education leaders …

SUCCESSION PLANNING AND PROFESSIONAL DEVELOPMENT

The first generation of founding CEOs is getting older. New professional courses have been developed including the NPQEL (National Professional Qualification for Executive Leadership), but we often find that those signing up for these courses have limited experience of working within trusts. Very often we find that headteachers of single academies and maintained schools are those who are enrolling and they have not all had the level of experience or pre-thinking required to benefit fully from the materials on offer. If we are heading towards a system of full academisation by 2030, then we need to be learning the lessons from the mistakes that we have made over the last ten years.

To do so we need to think carefully about the differences between the skills required to be a successful headteacher, executive headteacher, director of education and CEO. We haven't yet done a good enough job in preparing our people.

The ability to appreciate and to work towards interdependence rather than independence is one of the areas which sets the roles apart. The role of a headteacher is already well defined and in the UK, we have drafted and re-drafted the headteacher standards a number of times. The role of the executive headteacher or CEO within a MAT is much less considered and not yet fully formed. Perhaps the areas that come more into focus at executive level involve sophisticated collaboration, facilitation and political acumen. That is not to say that many headteachers do not already possess these skills, they just become more important and the leadership emphasis shifts as the family matures towards interdependence.

SELF INTEREST AND EGO

Too often, effective, strategic, educational leadership is influenced by over-inflated egos and self-interest. A recent memorable encounter with a CEO included a declaration that it was inconceivable that any schools within her/his MAT could be re-brokered into another trust; stating very clearly that 'if the sharks smell blood in the water ...'. When I inquired whether it might be conceivable that the interests of those children and families might be better served within another trust, I was met with an awkward silence.

This sort of protectionism is understandable; the stakes are high for leaders, but the stakes are higher for children. Of course we have to give trusts time and resources to make a difference; we know that school improvement takes time, and making decisions too quickly is rarely in anyone's best interests. However, we all recognise that not all trusts have yet demonstrated capacity for significant and sustained school improvement. This is something that is still not monitored effectively by all trust boards, or via external quality assurance. Intervention is too rare and often delayed. Children only have one chance at an education; time is precious.

BUSINESS OR EDUCATION?

The business of trusts is education. Clearly there are huge similarities between the education and business sectors, including governance and accountability. Yet the product, the outcomes and the moral purpose are different. Another CEO I met recently proudly talked about the fact that they had generated very high reserves over recent years. It was a relatively small trust and not all schools seemed to be doing very well; in fact, two had recently gone into Ofsted categories.

We had a discussion about what a healthy reserve position ought to be. I suggested that there is little point establishing significant reserves if the children in your care are not receiving a quality education. This balance of ensuring value for money and delivering excellent education for children and families is one of our challenges, but within that we have to recognise that our business is education and not the other way round.

FINANCIAL IMPROPRIETY AND LACK OF TRUST

In the early days of academy trusts, there were several high-profile cases of financial concerns, with many cases of notices to improve and ongoing investigations demonstrating how anyone in the system can abuse power and responsibility. The ESFA (Education and Skills Funding Agency) is still trying to ensure that pecuniary interests are declared in an open and transparent manner and that financial irregularities cannot occur, but there have been and no doubt still are occasions where interests are not declared or properly managed. It is not surprising that trusts established poor reputations though, as ever, it is the actions of a minority that tarnish the reputation of the system. *The Nolan Principles* (1995)[11] outline the expectations for public life:

- Selflessness – Holders of public office should act solely in terms of the public interest. They should not do so in order to gain financial or other benefits for themselves, their family or their friends.

- Integrity – Holders of public office should not place themselves under any financial or other obligation to outside individuals or organisations that might seek to influence them in the performance of their official duties.

- Objectivity – In carrying out public business, including making public appointments, awarding contracts or recommending individuals for rewards and benefits, holders of public office should make choices based on merit.

- Accountability – Holders of public office are accountable for their decisions and actions to the public and must submit themselves to whatever scrutiny is appropriate to their office.

- Openness – Holders of public office should be as open as possible about all the decisions and actions they take. They should give reasons for their decisions and restrict information only when the wider public interest clearly demands.

---

11   Lord Nolan. (1995) *The Seven Principles of Public Life*. Available at: https://www.gov.uk/government/publications/the-7-principles-of-public-life/the-7-principles-of-public-life--2 (© Crown Copyright 1995).

- Honesty – Holders of public office have a duty to declare any private interests relating to their public duties and to take steps to resolve any conflicts arising in a way that protects the public interest.
- Leadership – Holders of public office should promote and support these principles by leadership and example.

Not all of our leaders have upheld these principles. The system has not helped itself and that has resulted in many challenges and, frequently, a poor media profile. The general public are not all well informed about the multi-school system and high-profile negative cases tend to make the news, leading to biased points of view, often politically motivated.

The move away from local-authority control removed some of the reassurances the public had about the education system. It doesn't matter that LAs were not always successful, competent or consistent in their adoption of the Nolan Principles; they were a point of long-standing reassurance and the system has not effectively replaced it or fully secured the trust of the general public. Sadly, a number of trusts have revealed financial impropriety, lack of appropriate governance structures and conflicts of interest. In providing opportunities for entrepreneurial behaviour, we have given opportunities to people without scruples. It has not been good enough!

While we reflect, hold individuals to account and change the system, we have to do a better job at communicating that to the general public. There is a perception that the establishment of boards and the introduction of trustees has taken some of the 'local democracy' out of the system.

Historically, schools were supported and challenged by local democratic governance structures and this has not been changed by all trusts. Many have experimented with different systems of governance in an attempt to ensure that there is greater consistency and quality, particularly in relation to education standards, sometimes an area of weakness for local governing bodies. This has led to a perception that trusts have less accountability to local communities.

To repeat: it is in schools' best interests that they are effectively held to account, though there continues to be a perception that trusts are holding something back, perhaps trying to get away with something. Whatever the perception, networking effectively with local communities and local authorities, communicating with them and working with them, is in all our collective interests.

ASIDE

Question for system leaders

- Without formal quality assurance processes for trusts, how do we ensure that mistakes are rare and external intervention happens quickly in the best interests of children and families?

We have considerable work to do to demonstrate that schools are better led, morally and educationally, within families of schools rather than in geographical LAs. In part, this is a problem we have to own, ensuring that we are engaging locally with our parents and stakeholders, and communicating more effectively what we do and why we do it. Over time we must also ensure that robust quality assurance takes place.

NON-SELECTIVE

Most of England's trusts are formed from non-selective schools; a few grammar schools have founded trusts aimed at supporting local non-selective schools. At the time of writing, only 52 of 163 fully selective schools in England are currently in multi-academy trusts. (There are an additional 43 schools that also partially select on academic ability.) Among the 163, 92 are standalone academies; another 20 are foundation, maintained, voluntary-aided or voluntary-controlled schools.

During a visit to an East London primary school marking the launch of the Schools White Paper in March 2022, Nadhim Zahawi said that he wanted to absorb more grammar institutions into trusts, while still protecting their status. He also commented: 'their DNA I want to spread in the system'. Both comments are interesting in that they highlight some of the perceptions and, arguably, misconceptions about selective schools.

Dr Mark Fenton, CEO of the Grammar School Heads Association, has noted that some schools had been 'thinking seriously' about getting involved in trusts, but needed 'assurances' about their status. Clearly there must be some anxiety for grammar schools about losing their identity and autonomy, and for good reason.

Feelings about selection run high within the English system, with punch and counter-punch frequently played out in the media. We live with our histories and our prejudices. There are many trust leaders who would not consider welcoming academically selective or faith-selective schools into their trust, and would not be prepared to protect characteristics that they do not feel philosophically aligned to. It is a really difficult tension; having very different schools within families leads to deepening understanding between leaders and communities, parents and students.

However, if the philosophical divide is too wide, then compromise may not be possible.

Families of schools, by their very nature, highlight the lack of equity within the system. Local schools with local catchment areas can lead to middle-class parents playing the system, widening the socio-economic gap, with the ability to afford property in areas served by the most advantaged communities.

It is a self-perpetuating problem: we can all see the importance of having local schools for local children but it can and does lead to social division. When families of schools join together and staff begin to work collaboratively, they see at first hand the differences. It is obvious that the challenges in schools are different; no two schools are the same. We don't always understand the differences, of course, and we all accept that there are different pressures in different contexts. But if we are being honest, few would argue against the suggestion that life in secondary modern schools, within grammar school areas, is more challenging overall.

The anxiety about status is understandable. The debate about selective schools has been ongoing since the mid-1970s when most grammar schools were forced to become either fee-paying schools or state comprehensives. Any significant change to the overall system might, therefore, impact the grammar system. A number have embraced the initiative: in Birmingham, for example, the King Edward VI Academy Trust established a trust first by consolidating the five existing selective schools, along with King Edward VI Sheldon Heath Academy, and now an additional four secondary schools. It is a fascinating trust made up from selective, non-selective and secondary only schools, some single sex, all within a small geographical area.

In Kent, a fully selective county, the West Kent Single Academy Trust Alliance was formed in 2021. This is an informal partnership of schools, similar to the 'umbrella' concept. The alliance is not a trust, but is led and managed by a strategic board composed of the headteachers/ senior leaders of each member school. The strategic board controls and monitors the work of the alliance, holding regular meetings to determine the support that the alliance can offer. There is no hierarchy within the membership and the alliance is open to other schools joining over time. On an annual basis, there is a joint meeting of the strategic board (headteachers) and members (governor representatives from each school) to agree the strategic priorities and provide accountability for the work of the alliance.

There are many informal partnerships such as this throughout the system. This has been true for some time and there is no doubt that such partnerships provide advantages for members. Local solutions and models are to be respected. And if it ain't broke, don't fix it!

Yet in my view they cannot deliver the benefits available from a more formal partnership. Over time they are often reliant on individual relationships and their lack of hierarchy means that decisions, particularly more contentious ones, are difficult to make, limiting what can be achieved. There is no doubt that some have set this up to avoid formalising the structure and to avoid difficult conversations such as:

- Who will be in charge?
- What is our culture?

The limitations for me in this particular model are highlighted in the following website statement: 'The ultimate aim of the Alliance is to support efficient and collaborative school-to-school working.' I am yet to be convinced that this can be realistically and fully achieved through informal partnership agreements. They will come and go and may make a difference for a time but ultimately they will wither, depending on conditions, relationships and changing circumstances. Of course, time will tell.

DNA

What is also interesting from the Zahawi statement above is the notion of spreading the grammar school DNA. What does this mean? Presumably it is a compliment to selective schools, who clearly often provide positive outcomes for their students. Worth noting here is that only a third of 'outstanding' grammar schools inspected since 2021 have kept an unconditional top grade, casting doubts on calls to revive selection. The new inspection framework, coupled with the lifting of a previous inspection exemption for outstanding schools, has made life difficult for a number of previously 'outstanding'-rated schools. Grammar schools are more likely to be rated 'outstanding', but have not escaped the different expectations.

The downgrades are beginning to change the inspection profile of the grammar-school system.

In August 2021, 80% of the country's 163 grammars were rated 'outstanding', compared with about 19% of schools more generally. By the end of May 2022, this was down to about 74%. It is, therefore, easy to see why there is a perception that this 'outstanding' DNA is worth spreading. This DNA, though, can only be worth disseminating if it relates to leadership and teaching. If it is not to do with these intrinsic qualities of education, it must relate to other factors, other cultural influences on school experience: the outcomes, the students and parents, the community which teaching and leadership serve.

There is much to decide about what real partnership means within the system and any existing divisions are highlighted here. The difference between selection and non-selection is acute, and feelings run high. Parents also clearly have a view to which politicians are alert. Despite philosophical views to the contrary, parents may often decide differently when looking at the needs of their child. In designing the system, it would be naive to suggest that politics does not matter – even though, in an ideal world, it might not.

So, if selection is a good thing – and I am not suggesting that it is – and if the multi-school system is here to stay, then for the country to become fully academised we need to identify the best way of organising that system. If we don't, we will augment the existing divide between selection and non-selection.

ASIDE

Questions

- Should selective schools form trusts from similar schools or should they align with local comprehensive schools?
- Given that to gain access to a selective school children need to pass an examination, could grammar school trusts include primary schools?
- How might the completely 'grammar' areas, such as Kent and Buckinghamshire, best adjust to the new system? How should the partially selective regions adjust and organise themselves?

Society has changed: the perceived social-mobility opportunities and societal benefits selective schools provided in the 1950s and 1960s appear to be less obvious. The social divide seems to be widening with middle-class parents schooling children for 11+ examinations from an early age to avoid independent school fees. It is, and always has been, a political hot potato. If grammar schools are going to continue to play a part in our school system, how can we ensure that they contribute to closing the disadvantage gap rather than widening it?

ASIDE

Questions

- Should selective schools form music from similar schools or should they align with local comprehensive schools?

- Given that to gain access to a selective school children need to pass an examination, could grammar school trusts include primary schools?

- How might the completely grammar areas, such as Kent and Buckinghamshire, best adjust to the new system? How should the partially selective regions adjust and organise themselves?

Society has changed, the perceived social-mobility opportunities and societal benefits selective schools provided in the 1950s and 1960s appear to be less obvious. The social divide seems to be widening with middle-class parents schooling children for 11+ examinations from an early age to avoid independent school fees. It is, and always has been, a political hot potato. If grammar schools are going to continue to play a part in our school system, how can we ensure that they contribute to closing the disadvantage gap rather than widening it?

OPERATIONS

CENTRAL TEAM ROLES

As the trust grows from single to multiple schools, it is important to ensure that the central functions grow in response. In an ideal world, school leaders might focus more on school leadership and far less on administration.

Trusts vary in structure. Some retain core roles in schools, often keeping school business managers in place and deliberately having a 'light' central team functionality. Others go for a much more centralised approach, with school leaders being encouraged to focus on the business of teaching, learning and safeguarding. Again, there is no right or wrong way and schools need different things at different times. There are advantages and disadvantages with certain structures depending, for example, on the scale of the school and organisation. In some trusts this can vary significantly, ranging from small, rural, half-form entry primary schools to large-scale secondary schools. It is not a one-size-fits-all system and compromise may be required.

As organisations expand, the need for additional roles becomes acute: estates managers, PR, admissions, data leads and additional administration. As able people arrive, it can be difficult to imagine what we did without them. Organisations must consider the size and structure they are aiming for if there is to be intelligent design of central teams and back-office systems. If this is not considered, it can lead to constant restructuring and this is time-consuming and destabilising for all.

Many trusts have developed out of a single school and so the initial trust leaders often come from there. The headteacher becomes the executive headteacher, the bursar becomes the finance director and the office manager becomes responsible for HR and administration. It doesn't necessarily translate, of course, and there are different skills required for multi-school leadership which raises those recurring questions: 'what does it mean to be a trust leader?' and 'what does it mean to be a leader within your trust?' The different skill sets required for the job are not always understood from the outset. The difference between executive leadership and headship is considerable, as are the different skills required to lead the operational functions including:

- education
- finance
- ICT
- HR
- administration
- estates.

Those trusts that have grown significantly recognise that the needs of the organisation can change disproportionately. The ideal operating structure is better considered from the outset or, at least, well in advance of the need. The approach and associated structures can vary considerably, with divergence of thought often highlighted within the central team structure. All trusts have a CEO but not all have a number two in the organisation at the early stages and before scale is reached, preferring instead a flat structure often including executive roles in phases. In this structure, education is represented at the top tier of the leadership pyramid. Some trusts have a COO but where HR and finance sit within the senior team says something about an organisation.

Finance

It is interesting to see how trusts differ in relation to this function, some deciding to centralise operations and others devolving it directly to schools. Those who do devolve tend to retain business managers and this has advantages, particularly in smaller primary settings. It is surprising how many trusts continue for some time without setting up one central bank account, continuing to manage individual accounts for schools. Critical to getting it right, however, is one vital component: the finance director. Boards and CEOs need to make good appointments!

ICT

I have included ICT because so much of teaching and school administration is driven by its potential and development.

When I first entered the classroom well over 30 years ago, ICT was limited to the odd TV experience. A technician would provide a television on a trolley at the required time, hoping the VCR had worked. We might also have considered using the newly invented photocopying machine which did not always work (some problems persist). Computers were pretty new and not always to be trusted! Email didn't exist and we had to wait a week before seeing our photographs after sending them to the printers. Now we are struggling with how to deal with cyber attacks and wondering how we might benefit from artificial intelligence (AI). Recognition of just how important the digital world is to teaching and the running of school systems has to be at the forefront of trust leadership.

HR

As trusts grow, we recognise that one of the advantages is to take jobs away from educational leadership teams but this is not always possible. Schools still need to recruit, look after and retain their own staff. Leading and managing people remains one of the key roles for leaders within schools. HR trust support often becomes about supporting headteachers with the most difficult-to-manage issues: absence management, disciplinaries and capability. Headteachers who have previously used large and unwieldy external HR departments recognise the benefits of using a core team that they know well and that knows and understands the staff and their issues.

As we move towards a more mature system, there is a key question for us to ask about our approach to HR. How does the trust ensure capacity for improvement over time through:

- performance management
- succession planning (schools, central team)
- staff deployment
- recruitment
- retention

- CPD teaching, support, leadership
- rewards, praise and thank yous?

Some trusts have begun operating a 'transfer window'. This is an opportunity, at least once a year, for staff to apply to work in other schools and so gain experience and, often, promotion. There has never been a more challenging time in terms of recruitment and there are real opportunities for trusts to steal a march on their competitors. Within any selection process, in any school, leaders are encouraged to consider whether appointable candidates might, in fact, be a good fit for other schools within the trust. During the recruitment process, adopting a 'trust' mindset is beneficial for all.

There are some more detailed questions that we can consider when looking at jobs within the multi-school system:

1. Is there a consistent approach to performance management across the organisation?

2. How do leaders deal with under-performance?

3. How does the trust do rewards, recognition, appreciation and sanctions? How is this influenced by student outcomes?

4. Does succession planning consider all levels – schools, the central trust team and the board?

5. Is there strategic deployment of staff? How does the organisation develop its people and strategically deploy its staff to ensure that the best leaders and teachers provide targeted support where needed to add value?

6. Do staff embrace a culture of flexible deployment across schools to provide support where needed?

7. How does the trust manage recruitment and retention? How does the trust support its weaker schools in recruiting high-calibre staff?

8. Is there a clear CPD strategy for academic and central services staff?

9. Does the organisation have a clear strategy for the development of individual staff?

10. Is there a culture of continuous professional development where everyone is a leader and a learner?

11. Is there a systematic approach to training and development with ladders of opportunity across different aspects of the organisation?

12. How is the organisation improving the skills and competencies of its leaders and aspirant leaders from middle level to CEO?

Administration

As the organisation becomes bigger, the need for effective administration supporting communication becomes acute. It seems obvious, but too often leaders miss the importance of ensuring that 'office management' is efficient and supportive.

Estates

The country's schools are often in a poor state of repair. There are considerable risks in maintaining the portfolio of buildings and it is vital to ensure that there is a well-developed programme of maintenance, development, health and safety assessment, and asset management considered by suitably qualified professionals.

The following diagram outlines the need to grow with strength in pursuit of the top right quadrant: the scaled innovator.

Strong ↑	Chaos	Scaled innovator
	Devolution with nothing to provide structure as organisation scales	Quick to mobilise, nimble, collaborative
		Quick decision making. Empowered to act
		Resilient, learning from failures
		Continued fast growth and performance
		Healthy organisation
	Start-up	Bureaucratic
Weak	Free for all but works because still small enough	Too much rigid structure and process, and cost of getting things done stifles innovation

Weak ————————————————→ Strong

ASIDE

Questions for leaders

- How does the structure of the central team support leadership in schools?
- Are these roles vital, efficient and fit for purpose irrespective of which phase the trust is at?
- Has the trust considered the structures and roles it will need in 1–3 years' time?
- Are leaders putting in place these structures in advance of need?

If the central operations are not respected and valued by school leaders, the family of schools is doomed!

Effective trusts have teams working across schools rather than simply within them. Having effective people and systems which share knowledge and communicate routinely is critical. It leads to interdependence: 'school is trust, trust is school' is a motto many live by.

PEDAGOGY

Pedagogy is often defined as the 'science or art of teaching'. I think it is both and perhaps 'craft' would be a better word.

The 'craft' of teaching requires talent and ingenuity, creativity and forethought. It is a craft that can never be perfected; an asymptote (a line in maths that approaches an axis but never crosses it). Great teachers are always working towards that perfect lesson or sequence of lessons. They never quite get there. It is part of what makes teaching such a fantastic profession: we can always aim to get better but we will never really get to where we want to be.

Why is this relevant to the trust system? In relation to autonomy and standardisation, we know that many trusts have approached this in different ways, aligning or standardising differently. The question then is: to what extent should trust leaders try to align pedagogy? There are many attempts to capture and unpick pedagogy; a quick search will lead you to many scholarly articles. In 2012, Barak Rosenshine published a set of ten 'principles of instruction' that many educationalists have adopted and that I often hear cited in schools. In his book *Teach like a Champion*, Doug Lemov deconstructs the minutia of the craft. It is all important stuff and the research goes on as we constantly reflect, as we learn more and more about the brain and how our evolving cultural dimension impacts on the way we learn and teach.

CREATIVITY AND 'FLOW'

There is an understandable fear that by mandating pedagogy and practice we might inadvertently stifle the very creativity that makes it a joy. *Flow: The Psychology of Optimal Experience* by Mihaly Csikszentmihalyi is a much-admired work and focuses on absorption, the state of mind inhabited by people who become absorbed in a task. This task wasn't the finished work itself but was the experience of full immersion in the act of creation.

Csikszentmihalyi went on to study how people attained this state, and in his early work he focused on athletes and artists. He soon felt that this quality he referred to as 'flow' applied to people in many different pursuits, whether they were rock climbers, basketball players, hockey players, dancers, composers or teachers.

The danger, then, is that we take the creativity out of pedagogy if we try to mandate it, impacting on the 'flow'. Trusts recognise the interdependence between curriculum assessment and pedagogy but also know that aligning curriculum and assessment is much easier and potentially more productive, at least at the beginning.

The following diagram captures the challenge in that it is easier to move south east from the apex, considering first how assessment feeds into curriculum design. Many trusts have deliberately not dealt with the enactment of the curriculum, fearing that it might stifle creativity.

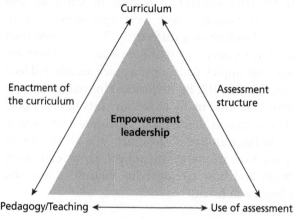

Empowerment leadership, reproduced with the permission of Dr Dan Nicholls, Cabot Learning Federation.

PEDAGOGICAL PRINCIPLES

Of course, some curriculum schema have inbuilt pedagogical principles. The first of the Rosenshine principles is to begin a lesson with a short review of previous learning. It is not rocket science and most practitioners would agree that this is a good start to a lesson. If a review of prior learning is a good start to a lesson, then we might argue that the curriculum content should be planned and sequenced based on this pedagogical principle.

In their book *Must Do Better*, Harry Hudson and Roy Blatchford call for teachers to be 'considered in the same breath as being an accountant, lawyer, architect or doctor'. We would, of course, be a little surprised if there was very much variation in the way that a doctor carried out their duties. Based on best practice and research, we would all be dismayed if surgeons around the world were to deviate too much from the playbook during an operation. Why, then, is this different for the profession of teaching? In part, of course, this is about the complexity of having 30 or so brains in a classroom all working differently. In order to make the right choices at the right time, a teacher has to become aware of the changes in thinking and behaviour of all the children in the room and that is a complex matter.

There is a difference between complex and complicated. Complicated stuff has an order, a set of instructions; complex is less reliable, and teaching is a complex craft!

So, pedagogy is complex and, as a result, any attempt to over-codify might result in the stifling of creativity, intuition or responsiveness. Whatever you do this time won't necessarily generate the same result next time. For this reason, many trusts have decided not to align pedagogy, reflecting on these lines:

> You can mandate to get the system from awful to adequate but not from adequate to great. To do that you have to unleash potential and creativity. This cannot be centrally mandated but has to be locally enabled.
>
> Michael Barber and Mona Mourshed[12]

---

12 Barger, M. and Mourshed, M. (2007) *How the World's Best-performing School Systems Come Out on Top*. Available at: https://www.mckinsey.com/industries/education/our-insights/how-the-worlds-best-performing-school-systems-come-out-on-top

Aligning or attempting to standardise pedagogy may be appropriate or more appropriate where schools need significant intervention and support: tightening processes in order to achieve adequate. Where trusts grow with schools that are facing significant difficulties, then it is often helpful to focus on unpicking complicated pedagogical processes. Sometimes teachers, departments and schools need to be given the instructions and to practise them before they gain the confidence to become autonomous.

To use a musical metaphor, scales are practised so that sight reading can become more fluent; there are common patterns which are helpful for musicians to become familiar with and these help them to be re-creative and creative. When we practise certain agreed classroom functions, it can help us begin to improvise around the classroom craft.

It is an issue all trusts wrestle with; the debate around autonomy and standardisation is one which all must consider.

In our trust, alignment has worked most effectively within primary schools with decisions about curriculum and pedagogical principles being agreed relatively readily by teachers and leaders. As this has matured, the curriculum content has begun to be adapted, local nuance has been added and content developed. The secondary experience is less straightforward and we will look at this in further detail in the Vehicle chapter.

The tension between primary and secondary is widely felt. There is no doubt that the generalised nature of primary practice, with teachers having to curate 13 subjects, leads to a more ready acceptance of standardised content. Secondary, single-subject specialists tend to be a little more precious about subject content. However, no one would doubt that there is no difference in the sophistication required in relation to pedagogy.

If we are really interested in disseminating best practice across phase (and I think we should be) then it would make far more sense to consider how the curriculum develops across key stages. While we do so, considering the best principles for implementation also makes sense. Understandably, the weakest systems need the greatest scaffolding, and schools in significant need of support benefit from having clear direction in relation to curriculum content and pedagogy.

If I had my time again, I would have begun the discussion about curriculum and pedagogy between phases much earlier. If your trust has schools in crisis then clarity around curriculum content and pedagogy is vital. If your trust is full of schools who are confident curators of the curriculum, then there seems little harm in beginning the discussion about pedagogical principles and developing a common language.

ASIDE

Questions for trust directors of education

- In this trust will the alignment of pedagogy stifle the creativity of the most effective teachers?
- If so, is this a compromise that is justified in pursuit of improving all schools?

The decisions around pedagogy will define the organisation and, to some extent, outline the culture, values and ethos. There is no criticism here, merely an observation. It may be that there is a difference between phases and trust characteristics. It may be that over time, those with the highest levels of pedagogical alignment are the more successful. Watch this space.

---

schools in significant need of support benefit from having clear direction in relation to curriculum content and pedagogy.

If I had my time again, I would have begun the discussion about curriculum and pedagogy between phases much earlier. If your trust has schools in crisis then clarity around curriculum content and pedagogy is vital. If your trust is full of schools who are confident curators of the curriculum, then there seems little harm in beginning the discussion about pedagogical principles and developing a common language.

ASIDE

Questions for trust directors of education

• In this trust will the alignment of pedagogy stifle the creativity of the most effective teachers?

• Is it is a compromise that I am pushed in pursuit of improving all schools?

The decisions around pedagogy will define the the organisation and, to some extent, outline the culture, values and ethos. There is no criticism here, merely an observation. It may be that there is a difference between phases and trust characteristics. It may be that over time, those with the highest levels of pedagogical alignment are the more successful. Watch this space.

QUORATE

Schools and trusts rely heavily on volunteers for governance, support and challenge.

They add so much to our system of education and they do it all for free. As trusts form, they do so with members who have the power to appoint the board. In a traditional company, this tier of governance falls away after the company is formed but in multi-academy trusts it remains in an 'eyes on hands off' approach to governance. In part this stems from anxieties generated from incidents such as the 'Trojan Horse Affair' which involved claims of an alleged conspiracy to introduce an Islamist ethos into several schools in Birmingham and beyond England.

THE ROLE OF THE BOARD

Traditionally, the board consists of trustees (board members) who represent different aspects of governance. Most have representations from useful professional bodies such as accountancy, law, business, culture and education. The board often splits into committees, usually around the following traditional areas:

- finance, risk and audit
- education standards
- human resources.

The board runs in a similar way to most corporate arrangements, with the CEO acting as the executive member. One of the consistent features of the trust movement is its inconsistent nature. Not all trusts have the CEO as an executive member of the board. I think it is helpful but not all agree!

The central change is that in forming a trust and installing a board, many of the powers formerly held by local governing bodies fall away. For most matters, the trustees become the decision makers. The challenge surrounding the system is what to do about local governance of schools and across the system, and different trusts respond in different ways.

The importance of having an effective board of trustees cannot be overstated; this interplay between board/executive team and the support and challenge created will define whether the trust flourishes or withers. The principal responsibility in the trust movement lies with the board and not the local governing body. This relationship centres around some critical areas:

- The role of the executive team in prioritisation, ensuring that the critical issues are raised with the board and debated thoroughly, and that decisions are made promptly.
- The ability of the board members to challenge critically and professionally, interrogating decisions but also supporting and adding capacity where required.
- The ability of the board to know when to intervene, but to avoid micromanaging; letting the executive team do their job but understanding enough to ensure that support and challenge are well placed.

In short, the executive team should emerge from a board meeting prepared to think differently about things, changing perspective following suitable, well-placed, informed, professional challenge.

KEEPING THE STATUS QUO

Clearly the board cannot have the capacity to look in detail at the workings of each separate school within the system and there is a temptation to leave local governing bodies in place. There are many advantages:

- Not having to restructure the system.
- Retaining good people who are loyal to the school and know the community well.
- Retaining the voice of parents in local governance.

The disadvantages often occur over time:

- It might become obvious that there is cross-trust variation with some headteachers not feeling like the local governors are challenging. Furthermore, headteachers within a trust system are accountable to the executive lead and can find that this replaces the relationship with the chair of the local governing body.

- The variation in quality governance standards is often most acute when looking at the degree of the educational challenge. Finding local governors who are well placed to carry out this role is difficult.

- The local governing body realise that some of their authority is lost within the MAT system and as a result they can become disaffected.

- Trusts recognise that the communication required between the board, the executive team, the headteachers and the governing body is considerable. There is a danger that this can lead to over-governance.

It is important to be aware of the key symptoms that local governance has become ineffective. Headteachers can report that they feel that they are having to inform their governing body about things and that meetings are a waste of time. They may feel a sense of replication; they may value the time spent with their line manager but resent the time spent with the governing body.

THE HYBRID SOLUTION

As a result of these disadvantages, some trusts have changed the articles of association for local governing bodies, changing their names to 'academy councils' and other similar titles. In essence this solution seeks to clarify who is responsible for what. In some trusts, the focus of the local governing body has changed and been reduced to matters such as local culture.

Where this is the case, the primary function of the AC (academy council) is to ensure that the school reflects the needs of the local community and protects its local identity within the family of schools. Through local observations and intelligence, the AC may inform staff and trustees of issues that will support their evaluation of performance. A number of trusts have also put in place school performance boards (SPB) with representation from educationalists focusing on a more streamlined agenda, dealing with curriculum, pedagogy and leadership. Where this is the case, the AC will receive feedback from the SPB to inform its decision making.

Academy councils might, therefore:

- work with the school, providing input to the periodic reviews of mission statement, values and strategic priorities
- support the headteacher in developing a school mission and values statement that is complementary to that of the trust, but which represents the differences of the school
- provide feedback on the application of the mission and values
- support the headteacher in developing and reviewing the school curriculum intent to ensure it is inclusive for the whole school
- challenge the senior leadership team/executive on safeguarding/ health and safety issues based on triangulated information
- engage with parent, pupil and staff forums to assess levels of wellbeing and satisfaction with the school/trust and identify opportunities to enhance the school mission statement, values and strategic priorities
- undertake observation and feedback on behaviour and health and safety issues
- provide governors to participate in hearing complaints, grievances or appeals
- receive drafts of allocated statutory school policies and provide feedback on how they are consistent with the school mission and values statement
- nominate governors to represent the school in trust sub-committees
- provide links with local businesses and the community to encourage support for the development of the school.

School performance boards might:

- visit schools and lessons, challenging the views of the leadership team on teaching and curriculum, reporting to an educational standards and performance committee
- approve the school budget ensuring that it meets the needs of the school development plan and priorities, including targeted funding
- consider the school health and safety, staff welfare, safeguarding, equalities and SEND reports, ensuring that the central team are acting on the recommendations
- represent the school governance functions at Ofsted inspections
- review school data and assessment analysis, comparing data across schools and challenging the central team
- challenge attendance and behaviour including exclusion trends.

Whatever the structure, many have argued that the role of local governing bodies in schools is not to hold trustees to account as they exist to execute the board's overall vision. Leora Cruddas (Confederation of School Trusts) has said 'governors on local bodies for individual schools in an academy trust are actually "committees" for the trust, and not mini-boards'. As such, they are not responsible for setting the vision and values and do not have autonomy within the organisation. There is no doubt that this varies across the system, with trusts promising governing bodies autonomy which may dissolve over time.

Ultimately there is a paradigm shift playing out here. A number of trusts have begun to adopt the phrase 'school is trust, trust is school' to emphasise the interdependent nature of the trust. We have to remember that the move from a single academy or local authority-led system and associated mindset takes time.

So a number of trusts have disbanded the traditional version of local governing bodies (LGBs), while most have introduced some sort of committee/council alternative. The challenge, as ever, is finding people who care about schools and the local school community, are willing to invest time and energy into challenge and support, but also:

- have a skill set that is useful to the system – such as expertise in finance, buildings, law, IT, PR, project management or politics, particularly local politics
- have a background in education at a level that can provide real challenge and support for senior leaders in the school system.

There is an opportunity to redefine governance within the sector. All trusts have charitable objects that define their responsibilities. Schools need this challenge but headteachers and school leaders have complicated and busy jobs. They need to be supported by clear governance structures that help them to survive and thrive. At the heart of this is working through the relationship between the executive structure, the executive principals, the CEO and the chair of the LGB or trust. When and if we get it right, we find a system which ensures that there is a clear remit, with delineated responsibility understood and supported by intelligent and informed volunteers. Bingo! If only it were that easy ...

ASIDE

Questions for leaders

- How do we make sure that governance is stronger as a result of the MAT movement, providing further support and challenge for headteachers and schools?
- Should chairs of governors be paid as non-executives are in the commercial world?

We ask a lot from our boards and local governing bodies. Should there not be an expectation that all senior leaders within trusts contribute towards governance across the system? Good responsible companies encourage workers to contribute to civic work through charitable objects. How do we incentivise educationalists to do the same ... tax breaks perhaps?

RISKS

All responsible schools and trusts have a risk register, and most consider it carefully in order to mitigate and pre-empt issues from occurring or escalating. We can consider a risk register as something we need to have or as a really useful management tool.

Broadly speaking, we can consider risk in two categories: operational and project. Operational risk management (ORM) is a continual, cyclical process involving risk assessments, controls and decision making. ORM is the overseeing of operational risk, including the risk of loss resulting from inadequate or failed internal processes and systems, human factors or external events.

Most educational leaders have encountered crisis moments. Over my career there have been several incidents: seriously flooded schools (twice), an explosion in a science prep room resulting in a significant injury for a member of staff, serious staff and student misconduct, sudden deaths of staff and students, oh … and a global pandemic. It occurs to me that I might be either reckless or unlucky! I list some of those events here because most leaders with any significant experience have experienced crisis incidents and it is really important to learn lessons after things have gone wrong. Given the high-stakes nature of accountability, it is understandable that we fear the consequences and become tempted not to air our dirty laundry.

Not all risks are avoidable but most are relatively consistent across the sector. The following sections do not make up an exhaustive list of risks, but each topic is worthy of a mention.

STUDENT OUTCOMES AND EDUCATIONAL PERFORMANCE

This is the biggest risk for trusts but it shouldn't be in the short term. The fact is that school improvement takes time and leaders are up against it working within a high-stakes system with an often-critical press and public. It can lead to some trusts/school leaders becoming rather risk-averse. Trusts are designed to make improvements to educational performance; the bigger they get and the more they support the system by taking in struggling schools, the more risk we add.

Most CEOs are concerned about the performance of at least one school but there are some where a significant percentage of their schools remain vulnerable. The bigger the trust, the more performance risks they can publicly take on. For a trust with 30 schools with a reputation for rapid turnarounds, carrying a number of schools is less of an issue than the trust with half a dozen schools that is still trying to prove its school-improvement credentials.

FINANCE

As the system matures and the economic outlook becomes even more bleak, finance is a growing struggle for many. There are pressures particularly on smaller trusts and on those with a predominance of primary schools where funding pressures are more acute. The scale achieved within the system is seen as the obvious mechanism for saving money but this can only be achieved if the trust functions are centralised. Soft federations simply don't help to diminish this risk.

PEOPLE/HR

For me this is always at the top of the list of risks. Recruiting and retaining the right people is the most important thing and this is becoming increasingly difficult. The terms and conditions for teachers remain very positive, with generous absence and sick leave placing increased burdens on school finances and significant cover required for colleagues who are not present. The supply agency business is currently unregulated, and relying on agency staff carries real risk and significant costs for schools. Headteachers know only too well what losing a few key staff can do to the school improvement agenda.

Emerging trusts are vulnerable. There are increased pressures when supporting multiple schools and the lack of scale means that we rely on good people who are often owning more than one brief. Before we get to scale, this risk increases and the reliance on potential single points of failure is something to be aware of. Large-scale trusts have a recruitment advantage with a pipeline of staff waiting in the wings to seize opportunities within an organisation they like and know. Good trusts have effective talent management strategies that mitigate some of the HR risks.

MANAGEMENT OF INFORMATION

In an age where trusts are being held to ransom by criminal gangs who seize control over data systems, crippling the organisation, the need to ensure that we protect ourselves and, importantly, train our staff to be aware of phishing is acute. There are also pressures of subject access and freedom of information requests. It is disheartening to have to remind colleagues continually about the importance of communication protocols, brevity and professionalism, upholding the principles of public life once again.

REPUTATIONAL

Like it or not, there are those who want to make life difficult for school leaders. Parents are, increasingly, much more likely to take their complaint directly to Ofsted. The press love a good story about unruly classrooms or corridors, bullying, race relations, admissions or poor Ofsted reports. It is relentless, and headteachers are having to deal with it via a communications strategy and through external advice and guidance.

The central team can really support here; it is another advantage of working at scale. We can share the learning and support schools through the crisis points of complaints and poor, occasionally irresponsible, reporting. The negativity over the academy movement makes it more likely that we will have to respond pro-actively, keeping our sense of humour and supporting leaders at all levels.

GOVERNANCE

The board is critical to the success of the trust. Where it works well, it provides high-quality support and challenge. However, it does not always go well and if the board, CEO and central team are not on the same page, it can prove catastrophic. Both sides need to have complete confidence and trust in each other. The dynamic between board and central team shifts as the organisation develops and this is a risky time. Board members' perceptions of a fledgling executive team may become quickly outdated.

HEALTH AND SAFETY/ESTATES

This is perhaps the most important risk for schools: the appointment of an estates manager across trusts is often one of the first to be made and for good reason. It is almost impossible to pick up all the risky aspects of estates during the due diligence process and there are inevitably 'gremlins' that appear. Small or single schools often struggle to ensure that they have sufficient expertise in this area and previously, they may have relied heavily on the support of the local authority. Now that this LA support is diminishing in some areas, commercial organisations are stepping in to fill the void. The move from the DfE towards the RPA (risk protection arrangement) insurance scheme has really helped; this much more realistic and supportive form of insurance in schools has been a real success, and this should be celebrated.

The questions which all trusts should consider are:

1. Does the trust/school have sufficient expertise to ensure that the schools are safe?

2. What are the human risks? In asking this question we are really exploring the organisation's culture and understanding. Most health and safety issues are caused by individual human error. The key, then, is to make sure that adequate training is in place for all. If something happens, then at least you can rest assured that reasonable measures have been put in place.

STRATEGIC RISKS

There are risks inherent in change and they can be internal or external. Any mitigation of these risks is dependent on an acute awareness of the forces, politics and circumstances inherent in a specific time and place. In short, trusts need to be keenly aware of what is going on and what might be happening around them.

One advocated principle of management states: 'It is easier to beg forgiveness than seek permission.' It is certainly the case that CEOs often have to follow this way of doing, in order to inject pace and to lead without fear or favour. That said, we live in a risk-averse era, so care has to be taken to treat risk with respect and proportionality – whichever of the above arenas one is working in.

ASIDE

Questions for leaders

- What are the biggest risks? How are these being managed and monitored?
- What external support does the trust require?

For those who are considering joining a trust, it is not unreasonable to ask to see the risk register. It is a quick way into finding out about the organisation, including the culture.

SCALE

As opposed to size – they are not the same thing.

ECONOMIES OF SCALE

Or, in short, the ability to deploy resources strategically across a number of organisations, to maximise efficiency while improving student outcomes and experiences.

'Biggest is best' and 'stack 'em high, sell 'em cheap' are not the most elegant of phrases but they accurately describe a business reality. This is the idea that as an organisation grows, it can create and produce more. The average cost of producing or processing each item of work then falls, so profits rise. If a store buys more of an item, it can negotiate discounts from the supplier, and can then sell them more cheaply than its rivals. Economists call this 'economies of scale'.

Economies of scale were the main drivers for the corporate gigantism in the 20th century. They were fundamental to Henry Ford's revolutionary assembly line, and they continue to be the spur to many mergers and acquisitions today. Trusts are not assembly lines, and educational objectives are not the same as those in business, but if we want the best for our children, then we do need to save as much money as possible so that we can pass that directly on to education priorities, people, services and equipment.

There are two types of economies of scale that can give organisations a competitive advantage: internal and external. When companies get too big, however, they can be hit by 'diseconomies of scale'.

Internal

In trusts, there are five internal economies of scale that we need to manage skilfully.

1. Technical

You can achieve technical economies of scale through improving the efficiency of what you do. For those in the trust system, this is about building on our experience of school improvement, developing greater knowledge and enabling workers to become more specialised and efficient.

2. Purchasing

Bulk buying can cut costs dramatically – from books to ICT equipment to contracts with suppliers. Of course, we all need to be buying the same stuff; it is not possible for schools to have everything bespoke. When we buy everything the same and in bulk, it perhaps takes away some of the unique character of schools. We have all heard some of the complaints about trusts who insist on the same backing paper and colour schemes. There is a rationale for this but it can be quite off-putting for schools who have thought carefully about the materials they use.

3. Managerial

As the trust grows, there is an opportunity to invest in expertise. For example, this might be colleagues developing their expertise in safeguarding by becoming the trust-wide lead, or the ability of the trust to reach sufficient scale to appoint an estates manager who has significant technical expertise. Growing slowly and scaling incrementally can be painful. The need for additional roles and gradual increases in human resource can often lead to part-time and fixed-term appointments until the organisation scales to a point at which specialist staff can be afforded. Often we see colleagues filling roles on 0.4 or 0.5 of a contract until a point when they can be given a full-time permanent contract.

4. Financial

The larger the organisation, the larger the reserves are likely to be and this means that individual schools can be supported more effectively if they go into a deficit position. Of course, this has always been the case

– LAs traditionally having to 'bail out' schools that go into difficulty – but it is a risk for small trusts that, for example, have a large number of small schools.

5. Risk bearing

The larger the MAT, the more the risk is spread. For example, in a large MAT, taking on a smaller school with a falling roll and a budgetary deficit is a smaller risk. The larger MAT might be more prepared to do this where, for example, there is an existing partnership network prescribed by geography or where there is a civic need. The decision for a small trust is much more risky, and the relatively small deficit might be disproportionate for smaller organisations.

External

External economies of scale occur when a company gains advantages as a result of events and developments in the industry as a whole, and in the external environment.

Many of us have attempted to predict the political winds over a considerable time. We all know that health and education tend to be the areas of public-sector services that are subject to political change in policy. Effectively, if you ignore this as a school leader, you are making a deliberate decision to limit the opportunities for the organisation. This is a difficult tension: there is the danger that we all work in pursuit of the shiny new initiative set by the DfE because it might attract funding or opportunity. Larger organisations, assuming they are quality larger organisations, are more likely to be trusted partners benefiting from opportunities as they arise.

DIS-ECONOMIES OF SCALE

Economies of scale also have a dark side called dis-economies of scale. The larger an organisation becomes in order to reap economies of scale, the more complex it has to be to manage and run such scale. This complexity incurs a cost, and this cost may come to outweigh the savings resulting from increased scale.

Frederick Herzberg, an American psychologist and business management expert, observed:

Numbers numb our feelings for what is being counted and lead to adoration of the economies of scale. Passion is in feeling the quality of experience, not in trying to measure it.

What is the trust trying to achieve? In answering that question, we might then look at the scale required to achieve that aim.

Experience suggests that the more collaboration and dissemination we put in place, the more trust-wide leadership roles there need to be. Doing more requires more resources, and more resources requires scaling up. The range of roles within the organisation is dependent on the central team income, which is dependent on the number of schools contributing to said income.

T. Boone Pickens, a geologist turned oil magnate, wrote about diseconomies in 1987:

It's unusual to find a large corporation that is efficient. When you get an inside look, it's easy to see how inefficient a big business really is. Most corporate bureaucracies have more people than they have work.

Size and scale are not the same thing. The size of a company is one of the primary ways to differentiate companies from one another. The scale of a company influences the amount of money it can typically generate, how it is structured, the geographical area it provides services to and many other characteristics.

Trusts scale in very different ways with many deciding to focus on back-office operations rather than pedagogical and curriculum collaboration and dissemination. The resulting structures are different as a result. In other words, there are those that have become quite big but have not yet achieved economies of scale either within school improvement or central services; big does not necessarily equate to being mature, efficient or effective. The bigger the organisation becomes, the more important it seems that it is successful. The DfE can ill afford large trusts failing, so the bigger they become, the higher the political stakes.

There are those who have structured to provide services over a large geographical area. Most have done so recognising the challenges inherent within the hub model, particularly that of ensuring schools are not left geographically isolated. Growth does not always result in a rapid scaling up of school improvement, which can often lag behind growth. So while we move to a more efficient scale, this lag in service improvement can become an issue.

Growth causes growing pains and those growing pains can limit the potential of the trust, increasing the risk at the same time. Those trusts that see the structure they are working towards can lay the foundations of that structure in advance of growth but this needs to be affordable and often it is not.

ASIDE

Questions for leaders

- How does achieving scale impact on school improvement and school services in the short and medium term?
- What is the problem we are trying to solve? What does the trust hope to achieve by working at scale that improves on the current level of service?

My prediction is that many, many trusts will develop into being large scale; over time, we are likely to have fewer but bigger multi-academy trusts. In order to really benefit from scale, trusts will look towards a *minimum* of 10,000 students. If not, they will be over-reliant on individuals and potentially become victims of circumstance.

TAXONOMY

As trusts develop, we recognise that there are various types, and it is important to recognise just how different they really are.

The Kreston Academies Benchmark Report (2024) categorises MAT sizes as shown in the diagram.

Small MAT
Fewer than 3000 pupils

Medium MAT
3000 to 7500 pupils

Large MAT
More than 7500 pupils

Classification of MAT sizes (reproduced from the Kreston Academies Benchmark Report, 2024).

LOCAL SMALL (200–3000 CHILDREN)

Occasionally we have seen trusts form but not really develop or grow. Mostly this seems to be occurring with primary-only trusts who initially grow to three or four schools but then do not continue to develop or grow, never really reaching a size that enables them to benefit from wider collaboration or economies of scale. Ultimately the risks are high for these organisations; they are often dependent on the founding leaders. Succession planning may become difficult because it is hard to justify the expense of an executive leader who is not working directly in a school and the job is less attractive for potential candidates without scale.

As the system develops, we all recognise that these trusts can become unsustainable, particularly when they are primary based. The funding required to put in place school improvement structures is always going to be a challenge, especially in difficult economic times.

We still see single-academy trusts across the system though the number is decreasing. In 2019 there were 1546 single-academy trusts in England; by 2023 this had reduced to 1222. However, it is difficult to see how this is supportive of the system and one might question the rationale for staying as you are. It is an important construct to understand, and we must try to see it from the perspective of single-academy trusts who would clearly prefer to navigate the system alone and with 'softer' partnerships. This deliberate decision in favour of independence as opposed to interdependence is not something that all leaders are able to articulate. Some value the agility and fear the loss of autonomy, and for good reason.

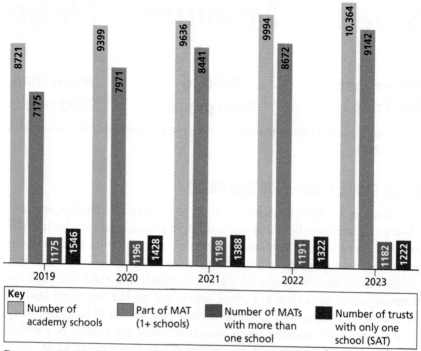

Data on MAT size (reproduced from the Kreston Academies Benchmark Report, 2024).

We also see some bizarre case studies, such as a trust formed of a primary infant and junior school. Effectively, this trust is formed of two primary schools, infant and junior, sharing the same site but coming together to form a multi-academy trust. Across the country there are numerous examples of co-located infant and junior schools bearing the cost of two headteachers where governing bodies and headteachers do not see eye to eye. It is the perfect example of parochial leadership gone wrong. It is very difficult to justify the extravagance of leadership salaries, let alone the time and energy spent on separate governing bodies.

Where small organisations take on schools requiring significant support, this can have a disproportionate impact on their ability to operate and requires considerable time from senior leaders and central team members. While they support one school, the services to other schools may suffer.

It is possible that small could yet prove to be beautiful and we may well see small trusts flourish, providing real benefits for the schools and children they serve. In doing so, there are a number of challenges to face.

CEO and board considerations

- Over time, it seems clear that there is an opportunity for trust leaders to make sense of the system. If the trust is simply too small and further growth is not possible, then there is a clear need to work with parents and leaders to develop much more sensible and cost-effective structures and processes in the best interests of children, regrouping and merging where appropriate.

- Organisations of this size often find it difficult to recruit the next generation of executive leaders and may be over-reliant on the founding executives.

LOCAL MEDIUM (3000–7500 CHILDREN)

A number of trusts have found it reasonably easy to grow to a scale of up to 7000 children, particularly if they contain secondary provision. At this point the trust becomes relatively secure but can often find life uncomfortable, not quite achieving the desired scale and related economies. As the system settles, it will be interesting to see what becomes of these organisations and we may find that there is an important place for trusts of this size. They are already playing an important role in the system, commonly taking on difficult school-improvement projects.

CEO and board considerations

- In areas with high numbers of academies, trusts of this size can find it difficult to grow, as options for local collaboration are diminished. As a result, they may see the alternatives as setting up satellite hubs or spreading the geography of the trust.
- As they expand, trusts of this size may find life more uncomfortable with leaders duplicating roles and fatigue can set in.
- At this point the MAT may wish to consider whether it needs to grow organically or merge.

NATIONAL MEDIUM

It does seem incredible but this still exists. Some trusts have been allowed to grow across regions but this growth has not been sustained, leaving certain schools isolated and without nearby support or opportunities for collaboration. For example a London-based trust may have opened one school in another city but that growth has not been sustained with no local hub to support. Trusts such as this may have overreached and will either be in a growth phase or be considering their position, looking for partners or, in rare cases, for a way out.

The challenge of serving schools that are geographically distant is not impossible and ICT has done much to break down the barriers of distance. Australian education has been working in this way for many years with students often unable to access full schools because of the vast distances that separate them from communities. Launched in 1951, the 'school of the air' involved lessons being broadcast to remote locations via short-wave radio. Written work and course materials were exchanged via the postal service or the Royal Flying Doctor Service. Advances in technology have meant that children in isolated locations in Australia can now receive an education online, but the lack of social interaction in this model can impact on learning.

The pandemic has taught us about the importance of informal conversations, but ICT can only take us so far and there is no substitute for personal interaction, forming and deepening relationships. The discussions over coffee and catching people as we move around schools create spontaneous connections; seeing people randomly reminds us to say and do things that we might otherwise have forgotten. School improvement needs to happen mostly in school; when we visit schools, we see the subtle changes to mood and atmosphere. The art/craft of school improvement is much more difficult to do remotely. Central team members who visit schools less often can be better placed to spot subtle cultural or behavioural changes. Change and deterioration can happen slowly and can go unnoticed by staff who become blind to shifts.

CEO and board considerations

- Where these trusts exist, it may be necessary to make decisions that are not in the best interest of the trust but are in the best interests of the local community.

LARGE NATIONAL OR LOCAL (7500+ CHILDREN)

The large national trusts are often the ones that are playing the most significant role in supporting the country's most vulnerable schools. Over the years they have gained the respect of the DfE, though some have fallen out of favour from time to time. They are all different in terms of vision, geographical spread, expertise and culture. A number have begun to develop their own curriculums which are then marketed as exemplars of best practice and support alignment.

In my experience, the medium- and smaller-size trusts are more likely to network and work in partnership. The larger trusts run the risk of not needing anyone else and may be less inclined to collaborate, though this is not always the case. There is a danger that the larger national trusts also begin to work together. For example, the Queen Street Group is a collection of 35 trusts that work together:

- to support and challenge each other as they continuously improve
- to help others to grow ethical trusts that work to serve local communities and the most disadvantaged

- to help form education policy.

As the system changes and develops, how we work collaboratively across trusts becomes a key consideration.

CEO, board and DfE considerations

- Scale brings its own challenges of communication and variability.
- How leaders engage with smaller local trusts is a consideration. The importance of making a contribution to local and other school communities is not always something trusts do, having network problems and priorities of their own.
- Where we have large local trusts, the potential for children and parents to have another option is limited. If one trust dominates a local area, limiting parental choice, then the DfE may wish to intervene.

MIXED MAT

It is likely that increasing numbers of trusts will move towards mixed-MAT or equity-MAT articles over the coming years, with an increased need to include faith schools, particularly within rural communities that might otherwise become isolated.

CEO, board and faith leader considerations

- The relationship with the diocese or faith body is important and it is not helped that many are taking different positions. How leaders work to preserve the ethos of individual schools is central to the task.

SINGLE-PHASE MATS

Primary-only trusts seem to be the larger group within this category. I understand why primary schools may wish to group together: there is an awkward dynamic between secondary and primary phases where secondary colleagues tend to dominate. However there is learning to be shared across phases with only six weeks separating KS2 and KS3. Collaboration over curriculum and pedagogy is essential and research development opportunities will be lost if we fail to work together.

CEO and board considerations

- How might leaders ensure that curriculum thinking and learning are informed by phases not included within the trust?

SINGLE-CULTURE MATS

Under this umbrella fall the single-faith trusts that are evolving across the country. In 2021, Gavin Williamson, the then Education Secretary, launched a pilot to support the establishment of diocesan academies. The pilot was established in partnership with the Church of England and the Catholic Church to boost the number of faith schools in trusts.

Nigel Genders, the chief education officer at the Church of England, said the scheme would 'improve the experience of hundreds of thousands of children' and 'further enrich the academy sector'. Church of England schools are more likely to welcome community schools whereas the Catholic MATs are keen to preserve the single ethos of Catholic education. Here there can be a problem, particularly in areas where there is no suitable home, and where schools desperately need support. In this scenario there is nowhere for struggling schools to turn and the only alternative is to hope that a trust forms nearby where they can be supported.

There are also trusts that are developing out of similar types of secular school. For example, there are those that have made something of a specialism, working within certain demographics.

CEO and board considerations

- One might argue that developing a family of schools with very different demographics and strengths ensures that best practice can be widely disseminated. Alternatively, we might consider it an attempt to be a 'jack of all trades'; in a trust where all schools are entirely different, collaboration may prove difficult.

ASIDE

Question for leaders

- Does the DfE have a clear view of what the system needs to evolve into? Other than the aspiration that all schools belong to a strong trust by 2030, what is the thinking behind system design? How can trust leaders best shape the future, locally, regionally and nationally?

My elevator pitch to the Secretary of State for Education might go something like this:

Please can we have clarity of policy based on some empirical evidence and sensible redesign parameters. In developing this please consult with the sector and think beyond the political term of office, gaining cross-party support. After considering and putting in place suitably robust quality assurance processes, please then let us get on with the job.

UNNECESSARY

How many activities do we undertake within schools and school systems that add real value?

The global McKinsey report (2010) authored by Mourshed, Chijioke and Barber entitled 'How the world's most improved school systems keep getting better', attempted to answer this question, analysing 20 systems from around the world to do so. All had improving but differing levels of performance, and the researchers examined how each had achieved significant, sustained and widespread gains in student outcomes. The report identified the reform elements that are replicable for school systems elsewhere as they move from poor to fair to good to great to excellent performance.

At the heart of the report is an insight into what interventions are common in effective school-improvement systems. Clearly all systems need different types of intervention at different points of their evolution; the following six are consistently observed in all phases of improvement:

1. Revising curriculum and standards
2. Reviewing reward and remuneration structure
3. Building technical skills of teachers and principals, often through group or cascaded training
4. Assessing student learning
5. Utilising student data to guide delivery
6. Establishing policy documents and education laws.

It seems clear, then, that these are the things to be developed as we evolve the school system. What, then, are the things that we should not get caught up in; things that consume our time and lessen our ability to improve as a single school or group of schools?

All school leaders recognise that certain external factors slow them . Such challenges – discussed in the following paragraphs – force leaders to identify and exclude the irrelevant, and to sort the 'urgent' from the 'important'. Accomplished leaders manage this adroitly; if they don't, they risk slowing down the improvement process significantly.

COMPLAINTS

There is no doubt that the number of complaints received by schools has increased since the pandemic. It is understandable that parents and other stakeholders become frustrated and there must be a process to make sure that schools and school systems are reflective, learning from their mistakes. The current system and culture, further supported by FOI (freedom of information) and data-access requests, place an increased burden on schools and trusts. This legislation, laudable though it may have been in intent, has the capacity to derail, distract and demotivate staff and schools. It can often take resources away from children, giving them instead to lawyers and complainants who sometimes don't know what they want or why they want it.

Clearly it is vital that we listen to complaints, reflecting and responding when we get things wrong. We must do all we can to ensure that complaints are easy to make for stakeholders with a genuine concern.

At the same time, however, we need to ensure that we do not give energy to those who seek to follow a personal and/or vindictive agenda, not always realising the negative impact this might have on an already fragile system and fragile leaders. One headteacher told me about a complaint he received from a parent on the first day of the summer holiday, a complaint he then worried about over the entire holiday. When he met the parent to discuss the issue in September, she admitted that she had been dreading the summer for various reasons and wanted to make sure that he too had a bad one! When September arrived, she felt inclined to withdraw the complaint.

BUREAUCRACY

We all recognise that with increased scale, we can increase bureaucracy. Schools can become obsessed with gathering evidence in support of measuring 'impact' and demonstrating compliance. In part, this might be a result of the increasing fear of inspection and litigation. Schools and trusts recognise the risks and the high-stakes nature of the inspection process and staff can feel the burden with increased requests for data, information, training logs and administration.

RECRUITMENT AND RETENTION

Too many good people leave the system, with four out of ten new entrants to the profession leaving within the first five years. As a result, schools spend far too much time replacing and recruiting, advertising and re-advertising, and interviewing for roles that were relatively easy to fill 10 years ago. The month of May has become an anxious time for school leaders who dread the knock on the door from staff requesting a reference or suggesting that 'they might like to try something else'. If we are unable to find suitable candidates, we are forced to restructure and attempt to fill in the gaps.

DEALING WITH COMPLEXITY AND CHANGE

Like it or not, and while accepting that it has many strengths, the English education system is a complex one. There is regional variation, of course, but there are also complex relationships between the following to unpick:

- Local authorities (with multiple different and complex structures)
- Multi-academy trusts
- Teaching school alliances
- Research schools
- Regional/national subject hubs
- Diocese
- Initial teacher training providers
- Universities
- Regional directors' office

- Independent schools
- Music hubs
- Voluntary aided/voluntary controlled schools
- Cooperative schools
- Local partnership agreements and MOUs (memorandum of understanding)
- Vocational colleges and technical schools
- Grammar schools
- Complicated admission systems and processes
- Middle school systems
- Free schools
- Academies.

There is certainly variety but one might argue that it takes a lot to understand and interpret the local nuances. In a trust movement predicated on collaboration, we have to spend time understanding the politics and relationships that lie within any local system, and it would not be necessary if we had not evolved such a complicated system of education. In common with experienced headteachers, creative trust leaders bring clarity and simplicity to complex relationships and environments.

SEND

We all recognise that the needs of our children have increased post pandemic, but while the need has increased, the funding has not. In response, some authorities have added layers of bureaucracy in order to access services or funding. Added to this, the lack of availability of educational psychologists, learning support staff and SENDcos means that we cannot focus on what matters most for our children. We are clearly spending time dealing with unnecessary paperwork and recruitment and this time would be better spent with children and families.

COLLECTING BUT NOT USING THE DATA, INCLUDING CRAZY WAYS TO MISUSE ICT

When we use data to inform our practice, it adds to the research base that informs our understanding of what makes for effective pedagogy, curriculum and practice. Very often we spend hours collating and processing but little happens in response. Middle leaders understand the frustrations only too well. We recognise that 'utilising school data to guide delivery' is an important aspect but we rarely do it well.

Increasingly, schools have data-rich pastoral and academic systems, but too often they do not talk to each other. Pastoral data that informs the pastoral system does not always speak to the academic, and all too often sits independently with pastoral leaders. Strong independence in relation to school data rarely turns into interdependence where all the data surrounding individuals is considered and acted upon.

More importantly, we all know how difficult it is to deal with complex safeguarding issues and the clear lines of communication, time lines and accountability structures that need to be in place to ensure that we keep children safe. A simple clerical or administrative error can have big consequences.

Anyone who has had to respond to a data-access request will have been horrified at how much educationalists respond and comment on email or social media. It is understandable; we care and want to help resolve things. We also get frustrated and when we do, we can become distracted from our core purpose venting our frustrations via email copying everyone in and pressing send late at night! Schools are on the front line: teachers and support staff have to be counsellors, nurses, carers, mediators, police and mental health first aiders. If adequate wider social and health provision were in place, we might not have to get so distracted.

ASIDE

Question for leaders

- How can the system support itself by reducing the unnecessary burdens of bureaucracy?

In 2005 the DfE sought to decrease the burden on teachers through the workforce reform legislation. Nearly 20 years on and teachers are still leaving the profession, in part because there is too much to do outside the classroom. If the prediction that AI will replace most if not all human jobs in the future comes to fruition, how might education harness technology to reduce the unnecessary?

VEHICLE

The curriculum is the primary vehicle for school improvement. There are others levers, of course, but for me this is one of the fundamental principles of the multi-school movement and one I did not fully understand or appreciate at the beginning.

In January 2019, Ofsted launched its consultation period for the new framework. By May 2019, schools started taking part in trials and the new framework was launched in September 2019. There is no doubt that it changed the way we think about our schools and their effectiveness – it is arguably one of the most positive changes that we have seen from the inspection system. Central to the framework is the 'quality of education' judgement, focusing on the curriculum's 'three Is': Intent, Implementation and Impact.

So why is this relevant to leadership within the trust system? The new framework puts the focus on what we teach and how we teach it. If the curriculum clarity, sequencing and delivery are strong, then we will/should see the impact. The main vehicle for school improvement then becomes the curriculum, improving teaching and leadership through that focus. The challenge, as ever, is how scale might better disseminate that.

The Harvard Business School produced a report in 2016 entitled 'The one type of leader who can turn around a failing school'.[13] The study characterised five types of school leaders within the English system:

---

13 Hill, A., Mellon, L., Laker, B. and Goddard, J. (2016) *The One Type of Leader Who Can Turn Around a Failing School*. Available at: https://hbr.org/2016/10/the-one-type-of-leader-who-can-turn-around-a-failing-school

- surgeons
- soldiers
- philosophers
- accountants
- architects.

The report studied the changes made by 411 leaders of UK academies: its findings suggested that the UK may be appointing, rewarding and recognising the wrong leaders.

It found that some talk a good game, but have little impact; some make everything look OK, but things are fragile and soon fall apart; some improve the finances but outcomes dip; and some make dramatic, swift changes that do not last. Critically, it is the 'architects' who have the greatest impact on schools and communities. These architects know that it takes time to improve schools, and they make sure that the environment is right for teachers and students by taking a holistic and long-term view. They may not always be the headteachers who are awarded prizes, and on average their pay may be less, but their legacy might be greater by far.

This is relevant because school improvement at scale also takes time. Too often in schools we are reliant on our best leaders and when those great leaders leave, we find that no one can replicate what they do. Often in primary schools, great teachers and leaders establish curriculums that are highly effective but that no one else can teach. When they leave a small school, everything must start again from scratch. Headteachers can always list the few teachers/leaders they cannot afford to lose.

The challenges facing schools are numerous and complex, but there are two great levers that need to be deployed by the multi-school system in order to improve teaching and leadership across our schools:

1. How do we disseminate our best practice at scale?
2. How can we make sure that this best practice is implemented widely and effectively?

The multi-school system allows us to generate insurance policies against hero leadership. Allowing too much autonomy is, therefore, a risk to sustainable school improvement. As a sector, we have not yet codified what we need to do to achieve school improvement at scale. It is about time we made the attempt!

When we began our trust project, we asked our leaders to plot their thoughts on autonomy on a line. We gave them cards to place on this autonomy-compliance line.

Autonomy	Convergence	Collaboration	Alignment	Standardisation	Compliance

The MAT improvement context (source: Cathedral Schools Trust).

Unsurprisingly, leaders placed most cards at the beginning of the line. The only exceptions were things like safeguarding and health and safety. Everyone placed 'curriculum' at the beginning of the line, clearly believing in the value of creativity and autonomy. Three years later we asked them to repeat the exercise – the result was radically different. All leaders had changed their view on alignment, putting most categories towards the middle of the line, firmly within the alignment quadrant. Why did this happen? It was not to do with any change of leadership; these were the same headteachers. What had changed to cause such a paradigm shift?

The answer lies in the collaboration work that had taken place in the intervening time, particularly in relation to the curriculum. This commitment to partnership had become much more important to them, and it wasn't all deliberate.

PRIMARY

In 2021, following a number of significant staffing challenges, one of our new primary headteachers recognised that the curriculum needed significant re-writing. After extensive research, he suggested the adoption of the CUSP (Curriculum with Unity Schools Partnership) for a number of subjects, and the central team supported the suggestion. It was difficult and challenging for staff, with a lot of work to do, but the early signs were promising enough for other schools to take an interest.

One school which had recently joined the trust needed some significant curriculum support and was sitting securely within a negative Ofsted category. Another single-form-entry primary school had had a number of staff leave during the summer term, leaving the curriculum in a fragile place. This school also decided to join the trial. Simultaneously, the trust appointed a primary curriculum specialist to facilitate collaboration; once the three schools were collaborating and demonstrating positive progress, it became tempting for others to join. Over a one-year period, all primary schools decided to come on board and an aligned partial curriculum and planning infrastructure were born.

Clearly the decision was co-constructed; this rather democratic style of collaboration brings buy-in but it also takes considerable time and energy. Trusts that are accredited sponsors have often had to take on schools in highly challenging circumstances and who need immediate curriculum support. This 'standardised' approach to school improvement via the vehicle of the curriculum is needed in these cases, and schools often cannot afford the luxury of co-construction.

SECONDARY

Within the secondary phase, our curriculum-alignment journey was different and less driven by urgent school improvement. The free school within the trust was entering its third year since opening, creating an imperative to choose a KS4 curriculum, and it made sense to use this as a lever towards alignment. One of the inherent weaknesses of free schools is that they are constantly doing things for the first time, and there is little or fragile corporate memory. As a result, it made sense to ensure that curriculum leaders were able to work with experienced KS4 teachers and leaders from other schools within the family. In order to do this consistently, we decided to unify the syllabi in time for the free school to make intelligent choices.

Consequently, the process was much less collaborative than the primary-phase project. We empowered leaders to make their own choices, but didn't give them a choice not to do it. It took longer for leaders to recognise the benefits, and there were some tensions to say the least. Not all were able to recognise the potential long-term benefits of collaboration. There were a small number of very insightful thinkers and pedagogues who just did not agree – they felt the loss of autonomy keenly. Not all stayed with us; it was a real loss of talent.

That said, we all recognise the leadership imperative to prepare the organisation for the long term – a time when they, and others, are no longer there. If you are determined to be an architect, then it is worth reminding yourself that trusts exist to add value over time and that to do that, we have to deploy a range of strategies that will make a difference. An aligned curriculum is one of those strategies and key to developing school improvement at scale.

ASIDE

Question for trust directors of education

- Is the curriculum the key vehicle for school improvement? If so, how do we address this within your trust?

If the multi-academy system is to be the consistent future structure for the English education system, then the paradigm shift between curriculum autonomy and alignment (albeit co-constructed alignment) is one that needs to happen.

To do so, we must demonstrate that co-constructed curricula can be richer than individualised versions and better stand the test of time. The problem is that some of our best curriculum thinkers and pedagogues are the most creative and are, perhaps, the least likely to adopt any prescriptive models.

That said, we all recognise the leadership imperative to prepare the organisation for the long term — a time when they, and others, are no longer there. If you are determined to be an architect, then it is worth reminding yourself that trusts exist to add value over time and that to do that we have to deploy a range of strategies that will make a difference. An aligned curriculum is one of those strategies and key to developing school improvement at scale.

ASIDE

Question for trust directors of education

Is the curriculum the key vehicle for school improvement? If so, how do we address this within your trust?

If the multi-academy system is to be the consistent future structure for the English education system, then the paradigm shift between curriculum autonomy and alignment (rather to construct) alignment is one that needs to be won.

To do so, we must demonstrate that co-constructed curricula can be richer than individualised versions and better stand the test of time. The problem is that, some of our best curriculum thinkers and pedagogues are the most creative and are perhaps the least likely to adopt any prescriptive models.

WONGA

Definition: Wonga: derived from the Romani word *Wongar*, meaning 'coal'.

Money is often one of the first topics we are asked about when schools are considering joining us and, in a time of educational austerity, it is hardly surprising. Some schools have managed to build reasonable reserves over time and may be anxious to protect them. Ultimately, it goes back to the short- and medium-term micro and macro tension, and we end up considering the key finance question:

What system over time provides the best service and education for children and families for the least amount of money?

Understandably, trust leaders are often asked the 'top-slice' question: 'How much do you charge and what do we get for the money?' Two things are worthy of mention, the first of which really raises eyebrows.

The point, we might suggest, is that it really doesn't matter if the top slice is 5% or 95%. If everyone can see the trust dividend, or the value for money, then all is well. If paying 95% works, the school is flourishing and children, staff and leaders are happy, then no one minds how much.

'How much does it cost?' is the wrong question, derived from the perspective that pervades the system: that somehow the school and trust are separate entities. It takes time to work this through and staff still consider that 'the trust' has money of its own. All too often we hear the question 'Is the trust paying for this?' and this can become irritating to central team members over time. Recognition that the schools are the trust and that the money is derived from the schools takes time but can be exacerbated by some common mistakes and unforced errors.

Queen among all of these unforced errors is a lack of transparency, often born out of a 'top-down' approach. It is true that local governing bodies (LGBs) lose control of the finances as part of the scheme of delegation; part of the resulting strength of the new structure is that LGBs (if they are retained) can then focus on teaching and leadership or community and stakeholder engagement. However, if central teams and trust boards are not transparent then it can lead to feelings of disassociation and resentment. For example, if a trust has a capital programme that has been carefully considered in response to need, but it is not shared fully with leaders or local governors, the perception might be that of inequality.

Often the true costs of support, initiatives or staff time are not shared with schools and, over time, schools can take for granted the offer from the central team.

In order to get to a better future, as leaders we have to imagine and shape that future. It is a paradigm shift; if trust is school and school is trust then we should all be working collectively to ensure that all of the needs are met and that schools are doing well financially. The relationship between schools and central teams (as opposed to trusts) is not merely transactional. If it is, then one might argue that there is something wrong in the relationship. Spending time in schools is important: talking to headteachers and governors about financial decisions through regular line management and HR conversations seems obvious but it doesn't always happen. Inviting local governors to sit on board sub committees, finance, risk and audit, for example, is an obvious way to ensure that information can flow both ways. It demystifies the budgeting process and builds trust.

Anyone comparing the relative top slices of different trusts must be aware that they vary widely. Some trusts include a number of services that others do not; some make an assumption that the central services will merely 'wash its face'; while others ensure that some top slice is put aside for a rainy day. That assumption from individual schools and staff that 'the trust' has resources of its own is difficult to shift and the concept that trust resources are shared takes some getting used to.

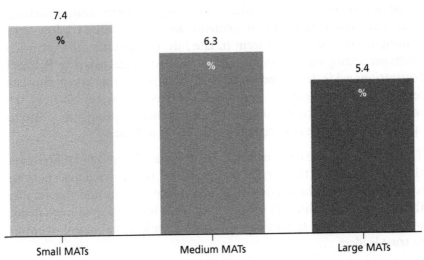

Central recharges as a percentage of GAG (general annual grant) income (reproduced from the Kreston Academies Benchmark Report, 2024).

We might assume that young and maturing trusts provide less in terms of financial dividend; as trusts mature, they seek to ensure that the financial dividend is felt equally across all schools. In order to ensure that we make a difference, leaders must consider a suite of strategies over time. Some of those strategies add value more quickly than others. For example, a new school, finding life difficult, may join a trust in order to make rapid improvements. As a result, the trust might deploy a disproportionate amount of money to make urgent interventions. If this happens, other schools within the family, particularly in smaller trusts, might be left a little more to their own devices and may suffer as a consequence.

Within a rolling programme of capital developments, some schools may require urgent intervention while others, with perhaps newer buildings and less need for intervention, may feel frustrated that they receive less investment. The trust financial dividend is something that needs to be viewed over a period of three to five years, and it is helpful if the central team shares that strategy with school leaders and local governors.

Over recent years it has become even harder to predict the financial climate, making decisions around school budgets and related staffing investment increasingly difficult. We all recognise the frustrations arising from late government announcements about pay awards (often now coming in the last week of term in late July, particularly difficult when trusts are setting budgets in May and June) and capital funding. Political frustrations aside, trust leaders do need to consider what an appropriate level of reserves might be. In doing so, we need to be cognisant of the moral imperative; the requirement to be financially prudent but also to spend money on the children currently under our care.

The following figure demonstrates the pressures on trust and school over time. The reality of the current picture is that primary schools continue to find life more challenging than secondary schools and the smaller they are, the more difficult life becomes. This is not a surprise to anyone working within the system and this gives an additional moral dilemma to trust leaders.

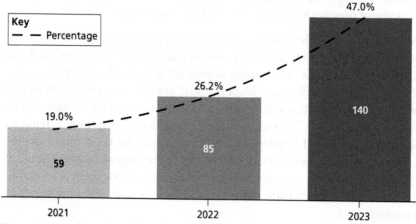

Percentage and number of trusts with an in-year free reserves deficit (reproduced from the Kreston Academies Benchmark Report, 2024).

The need for smaller schools to find a larger organisation to work within is obvious, but the tension is that smaller schools are less attractive to trusts. As financial pressures mount, the decision about whether to take in smaller schools becomes more problematic. The work required from a central team to support a one-form entry (1FE) primary school is not much less than that required to support a 2FE primary school but the income is half. The need for local, civic responsibility does not go away, but these decisions are easier to take when reserves are high. The decision to take in a small, perhaps undersubscribed, local school in need of support requires an understanding that other schools will support financially, and when those other schools are feeling the pinch, that is not easy.

This moral tension is one that the central government might not yet have fully grasped. The danger is that we end up with a high proportion of schools that represent disproportionate risks and for whom it is difficult to find a home. This does not support the policy of 'all schools to be in or joining a strong trust by 2030'. If we are to achieve this laudable aspiration, we might want to consider some incentives in support of that civic responsibility.

There is clearly anxiety about the future of funding for the system. The following table (using data from the Kreston Academies Benchmark Report, 2024) represents the concerns of system leaders about the medium-term budget implications. Based on their 3-year budgets, the survey asked leaders what would happen to their revenue reserves. Over 75% said that their reserves would either be lower or they would have run out entirely.

Average free reserves movement (£'000) (source of data: Kreston Academies Benchmark Report, 2024)

	2021	2022	2023	2023 reduction on 2022 (%)
Primary SAT	15	−40	−44	−10.0%
Secondary SAT	156	103	6	−94.2%
Small MAT	253	203	9	−95.6%
Medium MAT	644	372	40	−89.2%
Large MAT	1695	1564	267	−83.1%

As we work through the next few difficult years, the need for efficiency is obvious. Within more mature areas, trusts are now considering how they can work together to achieve even stronger buying power. This collaboration across trusts is becoming increasingly common; this was not the case with the local authorities where politics often got in the way of inter-authority collaboration. These fake political boundaries take little account of the relationship between families and schools, where schools often support children and families from outside the local authority. Commonly, local authorities made, and still make, decisions that take note of politics but not the reality of families and schools.

The following example illustrates how political lines can impact on budgets. I recently became aware of a school sitting on an LA boundary that took over 75% of children from the neighbouring authority. That authority needed additional school places and was asking local schools to take in additional students and offering capital enhancements to achieve this. Despite the school agreeing to house additional students, the LA then refused to fund it at the expense of families who wanted places because the school happened to be one mile from the border and in a different authority run by a different political party. The school was popular, successful and happy to accommodate additional students, but political boundaries and 20th-century thinking prevented sensible decision making.

Too often schools are overstaffed or proportionately have too many staff at the top of the pay range. Headteachers will always give you reasons why the staffing structure is required at any particular school. These reasons are not usually balanced or accurate.

It is all a bit gloomy out there and we need to make some bold decisions and work in partnership. Schools who are not full are finding life very tough and the statutory requirement for LAs to plan for places is a vital piece of work. They, in partnership with trust and civic leaders, need to adjust the admission numbers of schools to avoid falling numbers, closures and rising deficits.

ASIDE

Questions for trust leaders

- How can we ensure that anxiety about school budgets does not impact on our civic responsibility?
- How do we embed the understanding of how trusts and trust finances work for all who work within them?

It seems odd that we don't yet have consistent levels of funding throughout English schools and this permeates into capital projects, SEND and disadvantage funding. How much a child in England is worth differs across the country and this just does not make sense. There are always government plans afoot to balance stark regional inequities but achieving equity still seems to be many years distant.

ASIDE

Questions for trust leaders

- How can we ensure that anxiety about school budgets does not impact on our child reproducibility?
- How do we embed the understanding of how trusts and trust finances work at all who work within them?

seem, odd that we don't yet have consistent levels of funding throughout English schools and this perpetuates risks small projects. SEND and disadvantage funding. How much a child is flagged is worth differs across the country and this just does not make sense. There are always government plans afoot to balance school funding anomalies but perhaps an equal split seems to be many years distant.

X-FACTOR

The X Factor TV series ran for nearly 15 years and gave talented singers the opportunity to get a break in the industry. The panel of specialist judges was tasked not only with gauging talent but also with spotting something different in the contestants. Something that we perhaps hadn't seen before. Something that appealed to the audience and made them more interesting, more marketable.

My career started in music education and music was the reason I made it to university; it was my ticket into higher education. Once in the teaching profession, I was lucky to hit the wave of the specialist schools and academy movement during the early 2000s, initially as an assistant headteacher writing a bid for a performing arts specialist school in Southampton. I later became a headteacher in a new academy that opened with a music specialism.

MUSIC AND THE ARTS IN THE STATE SYSTEM

Clearly I, more than most, buy into the benefits for children of an enhanced musical and broader arts provision and the associated opportunities to develop social skills, confidence, resilience, discipline and enhanced cultural capital. These opportunities can have a transformational effect on children, particularly those from the most disadvantaged backgrounds. The same can be said for other specialisms that encompass the co-curricular theme.

Music and the performing arts are withering across the state system. The introduction of the English Baccalaureate, the worsening financial climate and the pandemic significantly impacted arts provision in schools and across our society.

The number of children continuing with music education after KS3 is diminishing over time, now approximately 5% and dropping by 37% since 2010.

- Only 27% of the government's target for secondary trainee music teachers was met in 2023.

- The target for trainee music teachers has only been reached once in the last 10 years (in 2020/21). Before this year, the previous low was 64% in 2022/23.

- 17% of professional music creators were educated at fee-paying schools, compared with 7% across the population as a whole. This matters because 50% of children at independent schools receive sustained music tuition, while the figure for state schools is just 15%. In addition, 85% of private schools have orchestras, compared with only 12% of state schools.

The quality of music teaching is inconsistent at best and this further contributes to the decline in standards and opportunities. In addition, the number of children learning to play an instrument or contributing to an ensemble is also diminishing. There is a cultural and demographic divide in music opportunities with representation from white and East Asian middle-class families dominating. It is a lamentable situation with a growing disadvantage opportunity gap.

As a trust, we are determined to ensure that these curriculum areas are supported and nurtured, but it isn't easy and it is costly. We have made some progress with significantly enhanced opportunities for all children in all phases to learn instruments and we have written curriculum materials in support of professional development. Opportunities have been enhanced by relationships with local music hubs and conservatoires but we have only scratched the surface of what might be achieved. The ambition remains and is a core part of our purpose; part of our reason to exist.

THE SPECIALIST SCHOOL SYSTEM

How does this relate to system leadership? Individual schools have often generated a reputation for certain specialisms, particularly curriculum areas; we all know the local schools that traditionally excel at sport,

STEM, drama or art. Often this arises as a result of the passion of a particular subject leader or headteacher. This reputation, this specialism, is not always sustained and may fall away when the passionate and inspirational leader leaves.

The specialist school movement advocated a system where schools developed specific strengths. First introduced in England in 1993 as a policy of the Conservative government, it was relaunched in 1997 as a flagship policy of the New Labour government. The system fell away in 2011 with the inception of the coalition government, but by this time, England had established a near-universal specialist system of state-funded secondary education.

Schools were later encouraged to apply for, and become, high-performing specialist schools. In this system, schools might apply for additional funding for other subject areas and for disseminating their expertise to support other schools. As with many initiatives, this political movement fell out of favour; it was scrapped and we moved on to other things.

The challenge, perhaps, for the current system is to ensure that real excellence within a particular discipline exists, and that it can be sustained and shared over time. Working at scale, we are more likely to be able to achieve this, and we should be less affected by the political tides, though clearly it would be naive to assume that we have absolute control. Scale should make us less fragile and less likely to suffer from initiative overload, initiative change and fatigue. The opportunity to do some things really well over time is not something we should overlook.

The school improvement landscape is complicated, forming and reforming as it has with teaching hubs, local music hubs, Maths hubs, English hubs, attendance hubs. In other words, lots of short-term funded hubs, favoured by politicians as being seen to react to the latest challenge in the system.

Clearly much of this is reactive, evolving in response to need and subject to budgeting pressures. The architecture of the school improvement system has changed considerably and trusts are leading the way, encouraged to work collaboratively in the spirit of dissemination. There is not yet a debate about how we might better plan the architecture and dissemination of expertise proactively.

While not necessarily advocating for a return to the specialist school movement, I am suggesting that we use the scale we have achieved to sustain excellence in certain disciplines. Independent schools have achieved this over a long period of time. The Music and Dance Scheme (MDS) provides grants and help with fees at eight independent specialist schools and 21 centres for advanced training. The scheme provides scholarships for talented children across England. In addition, England has an international reputation for choir schools. These are schools that prepare choristers for the professional rigour of singing within our great cathedrals. They are almost exclusively independent schools and government bursaries are available for these too.

It desperately sad and damning of our state system that in order to support talented children from low-income families, the government has to provide tens of millions of pounds of additional funding in support of an independent school system. Admission rules do allow for specialisms, and state schools in England are allowed to recruit up to 10% of students for subjects including music, languages and sport. The admissions code is clear, however, that these admissions must be based on aptitude and not ability. This is difficult to do and requires some form of testing. The administration of testing in relation to this is applied inconsistently across the country and there is considerable disagreement about whether we should be selecting in this way. The process has been challenged several times and the Office of the Schools Adjudicator has made a number of inconsistent rulings, exacerbating the confusion.

The process of assessing 'aptitude' inherently requires some form of specialist observation. In music, for example, I would maintain that hearing children sing or play is an essential prerequisite to the judgement of aptitude. Some schools, following an adjudicator's ruling, have had to resort to tests measuring the child's ability to respond to aural stimuli. It is akin to attempting to measure sporting aptitude without watching them run, kick or jump. It seems the politics around selection are relevant here, again pervading our system. As a result, we have to rely on the independent sector to support us in providing opportunities for some of our most talented children.

So what does this mean for the trust movement and for trust leaders? Perhaps there is an opportunity here to learn from the past and to use the new collaborative networks we have created to ensure that expertise is nurtured, harnessed and disseminated. We might make an attempt to develop real excellence in specific areas while, of course, ensuring that we provide breadth and balance. If we develop this over time and avoid being set off course by the varying other distractions and circumstances, we might then offer that excellence in support of the wider system. Perhaps then we will be able to offer places in support of talent to state sector schools.

The central question is: how can we make sure our trusts do not become beige but instead remain 'vivid' organisations? It can be difficult to achieve clarity about what a school or trust does really well over time, particularly when faced with competing priorities and budgetary challenges.

ASIDE

Question for trust leaders

- How, as trust leaders, do we ensure that new structures develop excellence that can be shared widely across regions?

The new teaching school network is a good opportunity to enlist the support of trusts. If we encourage trusts to invest in a 'specialism', then this may be a way in which support for the system can be more easily brokered.

Which trusts are exemplifying best practice in attendance, disadvantage and curriculum design? How can we learn from them?

YELLOW

Yellow? Read on ... see colour wheel, C-me!

The importance of teamwork is not something I have ever taken for granted. In my first senior leadership position in a comprehensive school in Southampton, I was lucky to work with a relatively large senior team brought together and galvanised by a school improvement imperative. All were committed, able and willing to go the extra mile. All went on to become headteachers. We were all very different and, of course, this was part of what made it a successful team.

At that point, my understanding of how teams worked was limited to a brief skirmish with the Belbin® profiling tool for teams, but that was enough to pique my interest. Looking back now, it was obvious that the Southampton team would be effective, held together by a headteacher who encouraged high levels of autonomy and creativity. The team worked effectively because the individuals within the team worked differently and appreciated each other's strengths. Over the years, I have come to appreciate the contribution of 'the team' and that is no less important within the trust core leadership team.

The start-up period for trusts, including the move from single school to cottage industry and towards a handful of schools, has many risks. Often there is a misguided assumption that if the headteacher had been effective in the single-school system then this would inevitably translate positively into the multi-school movement; this is not necessarily the case. The change from school leadership to system leadership requires a deeper level of strategic thinking in relation to people, change, resources and partnerships.

Headteachers need leadership teams that possess a broad set of skills and expertise. Expertise in pedagogy, timetable and curriculum design, logistics and, of course, relationship building. All schools need senior colleagues who have the ability to effectively de-escalate volatile situations, building positive relationships with children and families. Headteachers don't need to be expert in every area! The team within school is vital and can make a fundamental difference to school effectiveness. The skill set for a trust core leadership team is understandably different but also needs to vary, covering skills and expertise.

There are those who do not see the value in team analysis, but our experience has been nothing but helpful. Early on in our trust and team development, we enlisted the support of a consultant who worked with us on a framework. This enabled us to appreciate how each of us worked best and what we found difficult or uncomfortable. Perhaps the most powerful element for us was the enhanced ability to reflect on where we were all flexing our leadership preferences and, as a result, finding life/work more difficult.

The work challenged our assumptions of who we were and how we worked best; it helped us understand how we might work more efficiently and effectively as a team.

COLOUR PROFILING

The process we used was colour profiling, using a system called 'C-me'. Thomas Erikson uses the same system, categorising the colours as the four types of human behaviour, in his book *Surrounded by Idiots* (2019). He maintains that some insight into the way people behave is essential in establishing good communication.

During the first session, after explaining the process and after we had completed the questionnaires, our facilitator asked the team to guess the types of leadership preference. The system is based on four colours, as seen in the figure.

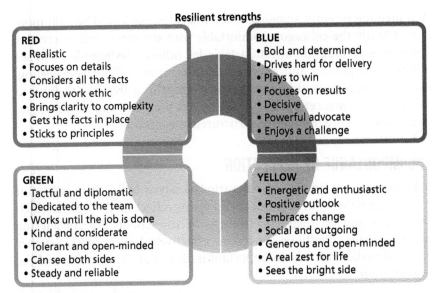

Resilient strengths

RED
- Realistic
- Focuses on details
- Considers all the facts
- Strong work ethic
- Brings clarity to complexity
- Gets the facts in place
- Sticks to principles

BLUE
- Bold and determined
- Drives hard for delivery
- Plays to win
- Focuses on results
- Decisive
- Powerful advocate
- Enjoys a challenge

GREEN
- Tactful and diplomatic
- Dedicated to the team
- Works until the job is done
- Kind and considerate
- Tolerant and open-minded
- Can see both sides
- Steady and reliable

YELLOW
- Energetic and enthusiastic
- Positive outlook
- Embraces change
- Social and outgoing
- Generous and open-minded
- A real zest for life
- Sees the bright side

The C-me colour wheel.[14]

The relative leadership profiles are plotted on the wheel, and teams then look at the most effective ways in which they work. What was interesting from the first session was that members of the team had made some assumptions about each other that were inaccurate; assumptions made based on both the person and the role.

For us, this has developed over time into a trust-wide profiling system. All our internal leadership courses now use the same system. As a result, a common language has developed and colleagues will reference the resilient strengths to highlight a team-related issue. In leadership courses we often ask colleagues to guess the preference and they commonly make an assumption based on the role rather than the person. The profile revealed that I was much more comfortable in the yellow areas and had to deliberately 'flex' into more uncomfortable areas. Our team incorrectly assumed my preferred style, but as no one was comfortable in the red zone, I assumed that role where occasion demanded it. I still do but at least now colleagues appreciate that this is a strain.

---

14   The C-me colour wheel™ is reproduced with permission from Colour Preferences Ltd T/A C-me. For more information visit: www.https://www.colour-profiling.com/

At a meeting recently, someone asked if a colleague 'could be a bit more blue'. Clearly the colleague, comfortable with the messy yellow creative space, was making life uncomfortable for others who were keen to see a little more process and were seeking reassurance. The free-wheeling, exciting, big-picture thinking was not something that was helpful at this point in the meeting. The colleague got the point and the result, no doubt, was a more productive, structured conversation.

THE IMPORTANCE OF REFLECTION

Whether you are pro or anti the various analysis tools, there is a point to be made here about how leadership teams reflect on the way in which they work and on their effectiveness. When schools are considering joining a trust, questions about how effectively leaders work together are rarely asked but it is an important indicator as to the culture of the organisation.

In his book *Belonging*, Owen Eastwood talks about the importance of telling stories, developing unity and establishing a shared purpose.

As trusts develop and we come to understand ourselves more and more, these 'stories' become important. Taking time to reflect and consider how we work most effectively is a part of the story. When a culture of open reflection becomes embedded, it helps leaders to be honest, considerate and informed, making the most of themselves and their teams. Leadership groups within trusts can include the board, headteacher groups, collaboration groups and local governance.

If a trust adopts a tool to help members reflect and better understand each other, then that gives space for story telling and also supports clarification on 'the way we do things around here', as referenced in the first chapter in this section. Teams that appreciate the relative strengths and weaknesses of their members work much more effectively and efficiently. As the organisation develops and teams change, it is essential that the working effectiveness of each team is monitored and such monitoring is only possible if the team dynamics are fully understood.

Let us not underestimate the importance of understanding team dynamics, particularly for teams that have evolved directly from school leadership. The executive function is different and the interdependence we are trying to create is new. All the members of a MAT team need to understand that and buy into the story we are trying to tell, the vision we are attempting to establish. Effective teams flex and vary their approach; they are reflective, open and honest.

How effective are your trust board team, central executive team and school senior leadership team? How you measure that effectiveness is important, and so too is what to do about it!

ASIDE

Questions for leaders

- To what extent has the trust considered the relative strengths and preferences of leadership teams?
- Is there a reflective culture within the trust and how does this support leaders to improve and work more effectively?

The way in which teams work within trusts is not always consistent. For example, it may be that the way in which the central team works is culturally different from the board or a leadership team within a school. This can lead to considerable tension and it can only be avoided by achieving cultural alignment in relation to leadership in order to engage in honest reflection and feedback.

---

we are trying to create is how. All the members of a MAT team need to understand that and buy into the story we are trying to tell; the vision we are attempting to establish. Effective teams flex and vary their approach, they are reflective, open and honest.

How effectively share your trust board team, central executive team and school senior leadership team? How you measure that effectiveness is important, and so too is what to do about it!

ASIDE

Questions for leaders:

- To what extent has the trust considered the relative strengths and preferences of leadership teams?

- Is there a risk to a culture within the trust and how does the trust support leaders to improve and work more effectively?

The way in which teams work within trusts is not always consistent. For example, it may be that the way in which the central team works culturally different from the board of a leadership team within a school. This can lead to considerable tension and it can only be avoided by achieving cultural alignment in addition to leadership in order to engage in honest reflection and feedback.

ZUGZWANG

Yes, it really is a word. Zugzwang is a situation found in chess and other turn-based games wherein one player is put at a disadvantage because of their obligation to make a move; a player is said to be 'in zugzwang' when any legal move will worsen their position.

For some schools this is how it feels. Many single schools now recognise the need to work in deeper partnerships but they also feel that by joining a MAT they might compromise their own DNA.

It does seem as though the time for setting up your own trust in some regions might have passed, particularly in regions where there are already high numbers of academies, such as the South West. Arguably, there are already too many and we are now seeing an emerging picture of mergers and acquisitions. So, if you are a smaller school and are finding life difficult, you might now be considering your options. It may feel as though whatever you do, it will not immediately improve your position. Zugzwang!

Effectively, single-academy or LA schools have three choices: remain as you are, form your own multi-academy trust or join an existing trust. We will consider each option in turn.

CHOICE 1: REMAIN AS YOU ARE

This is exactly what some have chosen to do in recent years, despite the erosion of services within certain local authorities. In some circumstances, this has led to a lack of partnership opportunities, though there has been an increase in the number of softer federations that have attempted to fill this space. These softer federations have not always invested in meaningful collaboration. It does take time and a clear and agreed remit for leaders to change and develop materials at scale.

We may find in schools lacking partnership that significant curriculum development work has not taken place. Isolation rarely prepares leaders well for inspection, though clearly schools are not necessarily isolated just because they have not joined a trust. Yet there is no doubt that many mature trusts have developed a sophistication of curriculum thinking underpinned by well-considered teaching and leadership development opportunities for staff. In well-run trusts, leaders understand well the concepts of 'Intent, Implementation and Impact' and can articulate it fluently, understanding the inconsistencies of implementation. Of course, this is also undoubtedly true for many schools not working within a family; I would argue that the conditions to make it work are more easily achieved within a trust.

Clearly this is not always the case and there are a great many schools that are in strong financial and performance spaces with positive soft partnerships. There may also be a strong local authority system nearby and the case for academisation and deeper partnership may not be strong enough. The government aspiration for all schools to become part of a strong family of schools by 2030 needs further consideration. We do not know yet what changed political tides might bring and we cannot predict the future accurately.

CHOICE 2: FORM YOUR OWN MULTI-ACADEMY TRUST

Our trust has grown relatively steadily, moving from one to 12 schools over seven years. Others in the same time frame have grown to three times that size. There are advantages to both.

On the one hand, getting to scale quickly means that you are not at threat of collapse or merger. However, growing takes energy and there are some trusts that have grown to scale without significantly developing the school improvement offer. Others have managed to achieve both. Developing the school improvement offer and aligning via collaboration without too much growth actually makes future growth more difficult. As the trust matures and decisions about alignment are made, there are fewer opportunities for joining schools to contribute and shape the direction of travel.

There is no doubt that some growth is easier. Taking on schools that require significant support is important, demanding and resource heavy; it is a moral imperative! Growing with free school projects is also particularly time and energy consuming and requires significant project management expertise and central team capacity. Taking on schools at risk of closure is important, particularly if they are local and partnership makes sense. It is all a constant risk analysis highlighting the importance of robust due diligence.

In forming a multi-academy trust, it is essential to consider the long-term plan and there are some pivotal questions for educational leaders and their boards to focus upon:

- What will the trust consist of? Will it include primary, secondary, selective, demographics etc.? What are the geographical considerations?
- What size and location are we trying to achieve?
- What is the purpose of the organisation, and why do we exist?
- What might the culture be: what is our view on the spectrum of standardisation to autonomy?

CHOICE 3: JOIN A MULTI-ACADEMY TRUST

My plea to anyone making this decision is to make sure that there is a cultural fit. This is not about whether we get on with the CEO, although that is a good start. It is much more 'about us'. What are the things that the trust cares about, and how is that articulated and enacted?

There are some who have considered forming a trust so that they do not have to join one, fearing that loss of identity and sense of self-determination. There are no doubt compromises to be made and there are risks, just as there are costs and risks associated with not doing anything. The problem is that we cannot predict the future, though as leaders we should make brave attempts and, frankly, are paid to do so. The crunch question – What is in the best interests of these children, teachers, leaders and families in the long term? – is one that governors and headteachers grapple with. It cannot be to do with self-interest, ego or politics. Decisions made by leaders today are likely to resonate for decades to come in their local communities.

So perhaps schools just feel a sense of zugzwang in the short term: staying put, forming or joining feels just too problematic, too risky or too scary. The solution, then, is over the horizon and, over the next decade or so, our job is to ensure that we make the case for new forms of interdependence, partnership and collaboration.

I have made the point that some form of detailed, long-term plan will support education leaders in making the right decisions for their communities. Leaving the development of trusts entirely to free-market forces risks playing to the worst sides of human behaviour and places pressure on leaders' capacity to adopt the Nolan Principles. If we are to get it right, we must provide incentives for civic responsibility and moral purpose, providing financial assistance by supporting schools that need it most and intelligently brokering the system.

The vision of hard-wired, accountable, collaborative interdependence is becoming established across the country. If this vision is to be realised fully, then we must learn from our mistakes, intelligently reform and legislate effectively. If this can be achieved then we will have successfully changed the way education is delivered and conceived, providing a blueprint for other systems to follow.

If you can buy into that vision and it resonates with your school, if you have weighed up the relative strengths and weaknesses of the offer and conclude that it is in the best interests of your school community, then I highly recommend testing the water and/or jumping in. It is an exciting and innovative time for anyone immersed in the business of education.

ASIDE

Question for leaders

- How do we ensure that all school leaders recognise the urgency of system evolution and their vital role in it?

A union official said to me recently that the objection to academisation was a battle that has been lost. The move towards the multi-academy system seems inexorable. We should all just get on with the design work, make some decisions and stop looking at the past through rose-tinted spectacles.

A school leader in a region with a high number of academies recently told me they were not in a rush to decide whether to join a trust. I reminded them that they had not been in a rush for the last 10 years and that in that time, the structure had been changing around them. They had not been part of that change and were not likely to be.

ASIDE

Question for leaders

▲ How do we ensure that all school leaders recognise the urgency of system evolution and their vital role in it?

A union official said to me recently that the objection to academisation was a battle that has been lost. The move towards the multi-academy system seems inevitable. We should all just get on with the design work, make some decisions and stop looking at the past through rose-tinted spectacles.

A school leader in a region with a high number of academies recently told me they were not in a rush to decide whether to join a trust. I reminded them that they had not been in a rush for the last 10 years and that in that time the structure had been changing around them. They had not been part of that change and were not likely to be.

SECTION
TWO

QUESTIONS

QUESTIONS FOR TRUST LEADERS

- What are the reasons for our existence and do we work in pursuit of that?
- Is our growth strategy thoughtful, supportive of the sector and in line with our mission statement?
- Do we operate in isolation or are we considering how to meaningfully collaborate with others and in line with our civic responsibility?
- Does our school-improvement model make a real difference? Are we closing the disadvantage gaps?
- How are we ensuring that best practice is regularly disseminated?

QUESTIONS FOR TRUST GOVERNANCE

- Does the culture of our organisation support and challenge our leaders sufficiently?
- Have we an agreed set of behaviours that ensure we all understand 'how we do things round here'?
- How do we make sure that we are recruiting the best people? Do we insist on external fields or are we constantly promoting from within?
- What is the appetite for risk in the organisation? Is this a healthy culture?

QUESTIONS FOR LOCAL GOVERNANCE

- What does your school need? Can that need be better met as a maintained school or as a single-academy trust?
- How are you ensuring that the curriculum is strong and secure, developing over time and well understood by all?
- How connected is your school to the local and regional system? Who are you collaborating with and will that collaboration make a real difference over time?
- Does your governing body understand the changing landscape and have they fully considered the alternative to the current status quo?

QUESTIONS FOR SYSTEM LEADERS

- Currently we do not make it clear via legislation what the purpose of a MAT is. We simply leave it to the system to decide. Do we need to legislate in support of this?
- If trusts have evolved differently, how are we sharing and using our knowledge to inform the next wave and to ensure positive evolution of existing trusts?
- How does intelligent brokerage take place? What powers are required to ensure that we do not continue to make the mistakes of the past?
- How will the next iteration of inspection take the pressure off headteachers and put the pressure on trust CEOs?

QUESTIONS FOR FAITH LEADERS

- What is the future of the church within education? What might it look like in 20 years' time?
- How can we ensure that distinctiveness is protected, developed and shared across our schools?
- How might the agenda of multi-academy trusts and religious bodies align in service of children and families?
- Should there be a consistent approach across the system and across all dioceses? If so, how do we get there?

QUESTIONS FOR DUE DILIGENCE – GOVERNANCE AND LEADERSHIP

- What are the key benefits to this school's pupils and parents of being part of your trust, as opposed to remaining a single-academy school?
- What vision does the trust board have for the size of the trust and how does the strategy ensure that there is the capacity to support additional academies joining?
- What is the optimum size and how will this better support teaching and leadership?
- How does the trust plan to build and grow the central team?
- What would the trust priorities be for this school after joining?
- What are the trust school improvement priorities? Is there a danger that we will not be a priority?
- What are the risks of further growth?
- Do individual schools contribute to the 3- and 5-year business and strategic plans of the trust?
- How are school admissions managed?
- What will be the role of the School Governing Body within the trust? Does the trust intend to implement any significant change?
- What steps are taken to ensure the Trust Board is suitably representative of the local school's communities?
- How does decision making work within the trust? At what levels in the structure are decisions made?
- Does the Board drive the governance structure, activities and agenda setting at local level or is this up to schools?
- How is the unique vision and values of each school in the trust maintained?
- How much autonomy do Headteachers and leaders have within the trust?
- How does the trust evidence effective working, avoiding duplication at different levels?
- How does the Board ensure that its governance structure is clear, in keeping with its Articles of Association?

- How does the Board ensure external quality assurance and support?
- How does the Board manage any conflicts between schools in the trust?
- How does the Board listen to, understand and respond to pupils, parents, staff and local communities across all its academies?
- What benefit do academies within the Trust draw from collaboration with other schools and other sectors, including employers, locally and nationally; and how is the Trust involved in contributing to improving leadership and schools beyond its own academies?
- How does the Board understand its academies' performance data, and how do Trustees know that pupils in all their academies are making the best progress they can?
- What mechanisms does the Board use to ensure there is a strong and effective executive leadership structure and personnel in place across the Trust with the right skills, clear line-management and reporting mechanisms?
- How does the executive ensure senior leaders within academies are challenged to improve the education of pupils, and what intervention would be used if improvement is not progressing according to plan at an academy?
- Do all the schools in the Trust have the same term dates/Inset days etc?
- Are there any potential concerns about this school joining the trust?

QUESTIONS FOR DUE DILIGENCE – REQUESTED DOCUMENTS

- Trust Articles of Association
- Trust scheme of delegation
- Governance structure
- Governors' Handbook/Code of Conduct
- Examples of communication with all schools
- Growth/vision/strategy documents
- Trust risk register

QUESTIONS FOR DUE DILIGENCE – FINANCE AND OPERATIONS

- Where does the trust believe its greatest trust economies of scale are derived from? Where are the cost savings made over SATs and LA maintained schools?
- What finance and operations systems does the trust believe are best centralised and why? How are finances shared across the MAT, and how are group wide priorities agreed so they are balanced and fair across all schools?
- How will this school see day-to-day financial impact on school operations through joining?
- Currently the trust draws a % top slice of school income – is this % of GAG income or all income?
- Is it likely that the trust will move to GAG pooling as opposed to top slicing within the next 5 years?
- What would happen to the individual school reserves?
- What are the spending thresholds for Headteachers/schools?
- What is the strategy around funding for SEND, Inclusion and Diversity – is there a central resource to support this in schools in addition to school's top-up funding?
- Reserves are? Is there any risk of diminishing reserves overall?
- How does CEO and senior salaries compare to national and neighbouring MATs?
- Has the trust got a large gender pay gap. What steps are being taken to close that gap?
- Does the funding formula change for a school within a trust as opposed to being a SAT?
- What measures does the trust have in place to ensure financial sustainability and stability across its member schools?
- How is trust capital funding fairly apportioned amongst the schools?
- What are the legal costs of joining the trust and who covers this?
- Is there any fact or circumstance known to the trust, that could affect the financial position of the trust in future?

QUESTIONS FOR DUE DILIGENCE – REQUESTED DOCUMENTS

- Trust Scheme of delegation
- Finance Policy
- Reserves Policy
- Management accounts for year ending and 2 previous years
- Accounts, Management Letter and Internal Audit Summary for year ending
- Annotated report to trustees for year-end position
- Summary of significant events affecting the business of the trust since the last accounts were prepared
- Latest balance sheet including assumptions around key reconciliations
- Detailed budget for next year and 3-year forecast
- Details of all services provided in the central services model
- Details of the centralised procurement process across the trust

QUESTIONS FOR DUE DILIGENCE – WORKFORCE

- Will our current school staff contracts and terms and conditions stay the same? Would new contracts be different to existing contracts?
- To what extent is HR centralised or localised? Contracts, staff absence etc?
- Would our school staff be on a trust payscale or continue with their own? If so, please can we see what this is.
- Would staff roles be 'at risk' through joining?
- Who is responsible for individual school recruitment?
- What is the immediate impact on staff of joining?
- What opportunities will be available to staff for promotion, management and CPLD? Would there be sharing of staff between schools in the trust?
- How is the performance management of staff conducted effectively?
- What level of autonomy do schools have in commissioning short term or long term agency staff?

QUESTIONS FOR DUE DILIGENCE – POLICIES

- Are policies (specifically HR policies but also all policies) centralised or localised?

QUESTIONS FOR DUE DILIGENCE – TRAINING, DEVELOPMENT AND WELL-BEING

- What are the core values and principles that guide the trust in supporting the well-being and professional development of teaching staff?
- How does the trust address concerns regarding staff workload, performance pressure, and well-being?
- Do schools joining the trust keep individual subject leader roles or could they be superseded by wider trust roles?
- How does the trust support and develop subject leaders with training, networking etc?
- What are the training and development opportunities for support staff?
- Do designated safeguarding leads have supervision? Is coaching or supervision in place for other roles?
- Is there a wellbeing support system including counselling and help line?

QUESTIONS FOR DUE DILIGENCE – REQUESTED DOCUMENTS

- The trust's current staffing and HR structure including any proposed changes
- 5-year forecast of the trusts staffing structure and succession planning
- Could you provide an example of the trust's communications to LGBs and staff?
- Could you provide an example of any staff surveys done across the trust and an example of responses with trend analysis?
- Current HR policies: pay, managing sickness, leave, staff handbook, staff well-being, recruitment and retention

- Please could you outline any major policy changes coming into effect over next 3 years
- Are there any potential reputational issues that the trust is aware of?
- CPLD process – how do all staff have access to a fair offer?

QUESTIONS FOR DUE DILIGENCE – HIGH-QUALITY AND INCLUSIVE EDUCATION: CURRICULUM AND ENRICHMENT

- Do we need to adopt a consistent curriculum model?
- With a trust wide curriculum, how is this adjusted to allow for individual school communities and school demographic? How will we be able to showcase our specific community through our learning?
- How does the trust promote cultural capital?
- How does the trust enable schools to retain their individuality and ethos?
- What additional facilities/experiences will joining the trust give our school's pupils the opportunity to access?
- What joint enrichment opportunities are available for the children of all the trust schools?
- Will our school still be able to continue to deliver its own enrichment activities – will we have the budget and space in the curriculum?
- Will our school be able to continue to develop its own creative curriculum?
- What opportunities are there for collaboration and showcasing within the creative curriculum? Can you provide examples of successful creative initiatives currently implemented within the trust?
- What measures are in place to ensure ALL pupils have a high-quality creative education?
- Does the church play a role among members and trustees of the trust? Does this have any implication to curriculum content across all schools?

- Will we be able continue to use the systems we have developed for assessment or will we be required to adopt trust wide systems and culture?

QUESTIONS FOR DUE DILIGENCE – INCLUSION AND DIVERSITY

- How does the trust manage inclusion?
- How does the trust manage diversity in the pupil, staff and governing bodies?
- How does the trust manage attendance?
- How does the trust support schools and SENDCos to improve the inclusion/SEN offer over what is achievable in a single academy trust? What central resources are available on top of individual school resources?

QUESTIONS FOR DUE DILIGENCE – REQUESTED DOCUMENTS

- Can we see examples of the curriculum model?
- Inclusion documents – PP strategy, SEND policies, attendance policies etc

QUESTIONS FOR DUE DILIGENCE – SCHOOL IMPROVEMENT

- What is the trust vision for school improvement?
- What is the culture of school improvement? Done to or done with?
- What are the key strategic improvement areas that the trust is working collectively on? What are the key priorities for our school improvement?
- Could you give examples of improvements in results for schools since they have joined your trust?
- Can you provide examples of successful school improvement strategies implemented within the trust and their impact on pupil outcomes?
- How does the quality assurance process work within the trust?
- How does the trust preserve unique identities and ethos of schools?

- Where there are falling rolls is there a strategy to merge schools and if so, what benefits does it foresee from this?
- Will our school still be able to remain part of other collaborative groups and activities outside the trust?

QUESTIONS FOR DUE DILIGENCE – REQUESTED DOCUMENTS

- School Improvement Plans
- SEF Templates

CULTURE

We began this book with a discussion about how we do things round here and the 'how' is referenced throughout the book. Communicating these expectations becomes the responsibility of all leaders across the organisation. One of the key roles of the executive leadership is to constantly remind all stakeholders of the mission, the vision and values, but it is also really important to record the detail. In pursuit of that, a number of trusts have attempted to record this detail in some form of leadership manual. Things to consider within the 'how we do things' section might include:

Expectations for leadership

- What activities and behaviours are **all** leaders expected to take part in and practise?

Autonomy vs standardisation

- What aspects of school leadership are consistently applied across the family of schools and where do leaders have freedom to innovate and improvise?

Behaviour and attitudes

- What are the consistent policies and practices applied across all schools?
- Are the sanctions and rewards systems aligned? Do exclusions tariffs match and is there an agreed policy and practice?

Business and operations

- What are the mechanisms for budgets, HR, ICT etc.? As an example, what authority do headteachers have for appointments and staffing decisions?
- How does the calendar operate?
- Do all schools have the same dates including training? Is there, for example, an expectation that school teachers and support staff attend specific training and development courses at certain points in their career?
- What management systems apply across the family of schools including software choices?
- What is expected in terms of compliance, including health and safety, risk assessments etc.?

Culture

As culture evolves and leaders become clear about why we exist, it is important to ensure that everything flows from this position. For example, when a trust is clear about its mission:

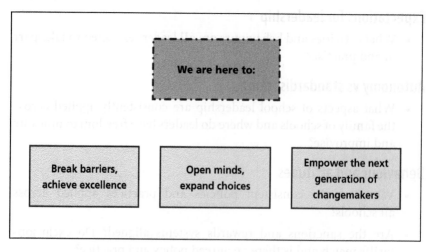

Source: Author's own.

When seen through the curriculum lens, this might lead to:

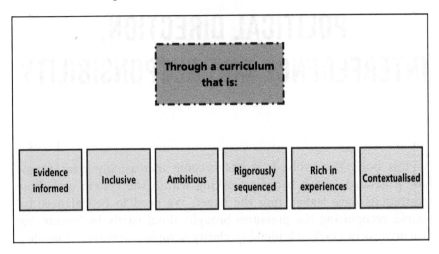

And as a result, you might have an aspiration that:

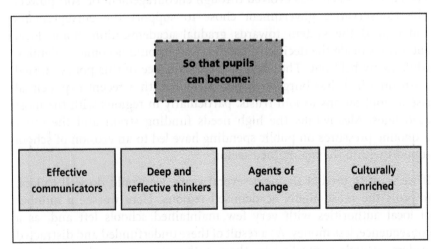

A number of trusts have begun to publish this kind of material to support leaders at all levels across the organisation.

POLITICAL DIRECTION, INTERFERENCE AND RESPONSIBILITY

As this book has evolved, it has become increasingly clear to me how frustrated I have become working within the system and those frustrations have leaked into the pages. We need to be balanced, of course, recognising the pressures brought about partly by 'events' but also because of a lack of leadership, clarity, scruples, wisdom or humility.

As the next phase of the trust movement begins, it will be important to understand what we might expect from any administration.

The current system has evolved through encouragement or 'soft power'. The Conservative government chose to support the entrepreneurs and cajoled the system towards gradual academisation. Some local authorities made the decision that all schools would become academies, while many held out. The inevitable consequence of this policy started a stream which has burgeoned into a flood with a recent exponential rise in applications to join trusts, particularly in regions with the most academies. Meanwhile, the high needs funding strain and the other economic pressures on public spending have led to an erosion of school support within the maintained sector.

If we want to predict the next several years, we would do well to look towards the most highly academised regions. Here we see a number of local authorities with very few maintained schools left and, as a consequence, less money. As a result of these underfunded and distracted leaders, schools controlled by these authorities are poorly served. In addition, many of those LA schools are less than attractive to trusts: they may be under subscribed, their infrastructure may be crumbling and, poorly funded, they often have a growing deficit. The system that has evolved through encouragement now needs clarity. If the future is not going to be fully academised and the intention is for a hybrid model, politicians will need to articulate how this will be controlled and funded. If the expectation is that we are to become fully academised, then say so and let us get on with it!

Either way, it will be important that the system is intelligently constructed. Wisdom is required and egos or partisan strategy cannot be allowed to get in the way of that. The system, be it fully academised or otherwise, needs intelligent brokering. Currently, schools still have a choice about which trusts they want to join. Headteacher boards chaired by regional directors influence and approve but cannot force schools who are not double RI (requires improvement) or are not inadequate in any particular direction. While this is the case, the design of the system will be flawed, subject to the vagaries of relationships and competition. If we are not careful, it will become very messy and require significant redesign. There are also likely to be high numbers of schools that no one wants!

My plea on behalf of schools, parents and children is to have some clarity. The next decade will define how our educational landscape will look for generations. I hope that any future plan gains cross-party support so that we can be clear and secure in where we are going. When we have that, we can make the right decisions to get there, better supporting the country's children and families.

System leaders have the responsibility to consider the vision. Too often, educationalists consider only the current, driven by the vagaries of political will and policy; it is difficult to think beyond the here and now. If we are to create an enduring legacy, we need to put the present climate aside and consider what we want the system to look like over the next few decades rather than the next few years.

SCALE, CAPACITY AND THE EVOLUTION OF THE SYSTEM

We looked at this in detail in previous chapters, specifically chapters 7 (Growth), 19 (Scale) and 20 (Taxonomy). As we evolve, we are learning about the relative risks, opportunities and challenges of scale. I have made the point that left entirely to market forces, to entrepreneurs, to self-interest, political perspective or belief systems, the shape of the sector would be flawed, disproportionate, overly complicated and marginalising. If we allow this to happen, we risk alienating the general public and also damaging some of our most vulnerable schools and communities.

Of course, there needs to be room for variety; a space where different types of trust can flourish and can fulfil a need. The same is true for individual schools; the need to ensure that they also can have an individual identity representing their community and vision. Safeguarding this remains one of the great challenges of collaboration and dissemination.

CIVIC RESPONSIBILITY

While evolution takes place, we are increasingly mindful of our civic responsibilities, including a consideration about how we might form partnerships with other civic actors. How, for example, can education work across the public sector to support children, families and communities more broadly? Some of this is already emerging with innovative schemes being launched across the country.

Schools are a focus point within communities. They are usually trusted. There are further opportunities to co-locate services. In Feltham, for example, the Convening Partnership is bringing together the local community, with local people, services and organisations working collectively and aligning around a clear set of guiding values and design principles. The partnership includes pre- and peri-natal services, faith groups, further education services, local authority, play groups, NHS partnerships and more.

There is a sense that we are all feeling our way a little. Some of the roles and responsibilities previously undertaken by local authorities are being led by trusts and other organisations. In part this has been brought about because local authorities are so poorly funded; organisations such as trusts are attempting to fill the vacuum. Post pandemic, where the fractures within our society have been widened, it has become increasingly important.

LEADERSHIP AND GOVERNANCE

Much of this discussion is built on the presumption that the sector can be underpinned by outstanding leadership and governance. Too few within our society fully understand the changes to educational policy and practice that have taken place over the last decade. One of the sector challenges is to ensure that stakeholders are given correct information that is not one-sided. Politics is always a part of what we do and we are not naive enough to think that we will ever achieve universal acceptance.

However, we all have a responsibility to ensure that our narrative is a balanced one. I have made the point that I am a part of the system and, as a result, this book sets out the benefits of the trust system but there is also an attempt to acknowledge the flaws and mistakes, and the challenges ahead.

Ensuring that the next generation of education leaders is adequately prepared and informed has never been more important. The paradigm shift towards structured interdependence is not straightforward; it needs to be interrogated at every stage of its evolution and by leaders at every level. Only then can we effectively disseminate and evolve the system to become leading edge.

RECOMMENDED READING

BOOKS

- *Belonging: Unlock your Potential with the Ancient Code of Togetherness* (2021). Owen Eastwood. London: Quercus Publishing. – This supports a good deal of chapter 1 (About) and some other areas of this book. It is very much about the importance of stories and stories take time to evolve. As the organisation develops, these stories define the culture.

- *Surrounded by Idiots: The Four Types of Human Behaviour* (2019). Thomas Erikson. London: Vermilion. – Some interesting reflections here about the different types of leadership behaviours as discussed in chapter 25 (Yellow). It is based on the C-me colour profiling system.

- *Centennials: The 12 Habits of Great, Enduring Organisations* (2023). Alex Hill. Wisconsin: Cornerstone Press. – In education we tend to think in the short term, driven by the vagaries of political direction. This book describes organisations that last and that think about things in the long term.

- *Frames of Mind: The Theory of Multiple Intelligences* (1983). Howard Gardner. New York: Basic Books. – This seminal work influenced much of my thinking both about how teams work effectively but also about how we ensure that the curriculum can provide a broad and balanced education, including considerations about the importance of the co-curricular.

- *5 Minds for the Future* (2009). Howard Gardner. Brighton, Massachusetts: Harvard Business Review Press.

- *Out of Our Minds: Learning to be Creative* (2011). Sir Ken Robinson. Chicago: Capstone. – Robinson's thinking about how the arts are not prioritised in education is well known. Trusts must make curriculum decisions and consider their priorities but we also need to consider how we are all encouraging creativity.

- *Drive: The Surprising Truth About What Motivates Us* (2018). Daniel Pink. Edinburgh: Canongate. – In this book, Daniel Pink discusses what really motivates people. He asserts that the secret to high performance and satisfaction – at work, at school and at home – is the deeply human need to direct our own lives, to learn and create new things, and to do better by ourselves and our world. It speaks to the civic duty referenced throughout this book.

- *Must Do Better: How to Improve the Image of Teaching and Why it Matters* (2022). Harry Hudson and Roy Blatchford. Woodbridge: John Catt.

- *Flow: The Psychology of Optimal Experience* (1989). Mihaly Csikszentmihalyi. New York: Harper. – I reference this book when discussing the tension between alignment and creativity.

- *Being the CEO: The Six Dimensions of Organisational Leadership* (2019). Michael Pain. Woodbridge: John Catt.

- *Experiential Learning: Experience as the Source of Learning and Development* (1983). David A. Kolb. New Jersey: Prentice Hall.

- *The Reflective Practitioner: How Professionals Think in Action* (1991). Donald A. Schon. New York: Taylor and Francis.

- *The One Type of Leader Who Can Turn Around a Failing School* (2016). Alex Hill, Liz Mellon, Benjamin Laker and Jules Goddard. The Harvard Business Review. – I reference this in the chapter (Vehicle) in relation to the time it takes to develop curriculum-led school improvement.

- *Fractured* (2021). Jon Yates. Manchester: HarperNorth. – This really interesting book looks at why society is polarised and why 'people like me' flock together. It is a reminder that trusts have a role to play in engineering community interactions.

- *The Advantage: Why Organizational Health Trumps Everything Else in Business* (2012) Patrick M. Lencioni. New Jersey: Jossey Bass. –

I reference Lencioni's *The Advantage* in the first chapter (About) but also throughout in relation to how we think about culture and teams.

- *The Five Dysfunctions of a Team: A Leadership Fable* (2002) Patrick M. Lencioni. New Jersey: John Wiley & Sons.
- *Knowledge and the Future School: Curriculum and Social Justice* (2014). Young, M., Lambert, D., Roberts, C. et al. London: Bloomsbury.

DOCUMENTS, ARTICLES AND BLOG POSTS

- *Our Hope for a Flourishing Schools System: Deeply Christian, Serving the Common Good* (2023). Church of England Education Office. Available at: https://www.churchofengland.org/sites/default/files/2023-06/our-hope-for-a-flourishing-schools-system-report.pdf.
- *The MAT Assurance Framework* (2015). Available at: https://assets.publishing.service.gov.uk/media/60a3c20ee90e0735799d7ff9/MAT_Assurance_Framework.pdf – Developed by leaders across the South West, this framework attempts to capture the qualities that define effective trusts.
- *A Self-improving School System: Towards Maturity* (2012). David H. Hargreaves, Wolfson College, Cambridge. National College for School Leadership. – This thinkpiece concentrates on the nature of deep partnerships between schools and the action needed to achieve them. It discusses the challenges of initiating and maintaining partnerships or alliances between schools.
- *How the World's Most Improved School Systems Keep Getting Better* (2010). Mona Mourshed, Chinezi Chijioke and Michael Barber. Available at: https://www.mckinsey.com/industries/education/our-insights/how-the-worlds-most-improved-school-systems-keep-getting-better
- *How the World's Best-performing School Systems Come Out on Top* (2007). Michael Barber and Mona Mourshed. Available at: https://www.mckinsey.com/industries/education/our-insights/how-the-worlds-best-performing-school-systems-come-out-on-top

- *Academies Regulatory and Commissioning Review: Policy Paper* (2023). Available at: https://www.gov.uk/government/publications/academies-regulatory-and-commissioning-review

- *What is a Strong Trust? A CST Discussion Paper* (2022). Leora Cruddas. Nottingham: Confederation of School Trusts. Available at: https://icm.cstuk.org.uk/assets/pdfs/ICE_10102_CST_What_Is_A_Strong_Trust_Discussion%20Paper2.pdf

- *Power Grab: Academisation and the Threat to Secular Education* (2020). National Secular Society. Available at: https://www.secularism.org.uk/uploads/power-grab-academisation-and-the-threat-to-secular-education.pdf – I have included this rather one-sided report in the interest of balance.

- *Ted Wragg Trust Leadership Handbook* (2023). – The Ted Wragg Trust, based in the South West, has captured its thinking clearly. There are many other examples but this is worth including.

- Tuckman, B.W. (1965). 'Developmental sequence in small groups.' *Psychological Bulletin.* 63: pp. 384–99.

- *Five Functions of a strong Trust | strong Trust, great schools* (2023). Available at: https://dannicholls1.com/2023/02/26/five-functions-of-a-strong-trust-strong-trust-great-schools/

- *Seeking a Trust Dividend | exploiting the power of collaboration* (2023). Available at: https://dannicholls1.com/2023/02/12/seeking-a-trust-dividend-exploiting-the-power-of-collaboration/

- Lemov, D. (2021). *Teach Like a Champion.* Published by: Jossey-Bass.

The A—Z series focuses on the 'fun and fundamentals' of what's happening in primary, special and secondary schools today. Each title is written by a leading practitioner, adopting a series approach of reflection, advice and provocation.

As a group of authors with a strong belief in the power of education to shape and change young people's lives, we hope teachers and leaders in the UK and internationally enjoy what we have to say.

Roy Blatchford, series editor